DON'T ASK ME SH#% ABOUT MARRIAGE

By: Christopher L. Lyles, Sr.

ISBN: 979-8-218-59649-1

LCCN: 2025904574

Limits of Liability and Disclaimer of Warranty

The author and publisher shall not be liable for your misuse of this material. This book is strictly for informational and educational purposes.

Warning – Disclaimer

The purpose of this book is to educate and entertain. The author and/or publisher do not guarantee that anyone following these techniques, suggestions,

To place a bulk order for your marriage retreat, conference, or workshop, please contact the author directly via his website, visit: www.dontaskmeaboutmarriage.com.

Table of Contents

Dedication

I dedicate this book to my Addiah. You not only gave me the courage to do this project, but you also spoke life into it; you spoke life into me. You surpassed my wildest dreams from the moment you opened that door. You have supported the whispers of my heart in a way that's made me believe in the impossible. I am eternally grateful to God for you.

Acknowledgments

I would first like to thank and acknowledge my Lord and Savior, Jesus Christ. My life is not my own. To you, I belong. Before I was in my mother's womb you knew me. You love me beyond my capacity to understand. All I have needed thy hand has provided. Thank you for your presence in my life.

Next, I'd like to thank my best friend and beautiful wife, Nikimi, for her love and support. You are one of my greatest cheerleaders and, without question, the finest! Your inspiration has been a fresh breath in my body. I don't know why God allowed our paths to cross, but every day, I'm thankful for you. You love me just as I am. You pray for and over me and allow me to cover you. Thank you for being more than I could have ever hoped for.

Shout-out to our tribe, Chris Jr, Jordan, Landyn, Anaiya, and Keagan (listed in the order God blessed me to meet you – not oldest to youngest). I've tried to be the best father I can and have discovered learning from you has been my greatest teacher. There is no blueprint to follow because you are all incredible and unique. It has been an absolute joy watching you root and grow. While this book is my personal experience, I'm constantly mindful and sensitive to what these experiences have been for you. I thank God for your resilience and patience with me as we have been figuring it all out together. Love you forever.

I'd like to thank my parents: my mother, Christine, my "Pops" Charles; and my dad, Alonzo "Rudy." Momma, you have been my shining example of consistent and unconditional love and determination. I will never be able to repay you for the life you provided for me and every sacrifice you made along the way. I thank God for all three of you for always showing up for me in your ways. Without each of you, there is no me. For this, and you, I am forever and truly grateful.

To my baby sister Charnetta and other siblings (thicker than blood), my in-laws, aunts, uncles, nieces, nephews, and cousins, I love you all and thank you for allowing me space in your lives and hearts. I didn't choose my family, but I'm thankful God chose you for me.

To my brothers past and present, thank you for being my sounding boards, shoulders to lean on, and having my back. Although I didn't have biological brothers, you were all I had when the nights got dark for your boy. I'm forever grateful that you saw through my mask and put money in my hands when I didn't have it. You gave me a place to sleep when I didn't have one. You fed and encouraged me when I didn't have the strength to do it myself. You called right when I was about to do something stupid. You saved my life. Thank you!

To my pastor, Walter Lee Bowers, Jr., and my entire Chosen City Church family, thank you for allowing me to serve with and alongside each of you. I'm humbled to be your brother and grateful you won't let a few cuss words come between us! LOL! "We've been CHOSEN for the city!"

To Bishop William H. Woodard Jr., and Pastor Wilse Sample, Jr., thank you for being who God called you to be the spiritual extension of my natural fathers. Your love, wisdom, and guidance have been immeasurable, and I am forever grateful. For the record, I know you don't condone many of the decisions I've made throughout the years, but thank you for still answering when I call, like a loving father always does.

To my writing coach, Tamika, of Ink Pen Diva, thank you for the directions, encouragement, and stern correction. Your vision and leadership are next level. You helped bring my thoughts and experiences to life. Thank you for blessing us with your gift and passion for writing and coaching. Hornets 4Life!

To my ex-wives, while I don't regret the past, I am mindful of the processes we've gone through to heal. No one wants or expects to have scars from relationships, but they do occur; therefore,

I have and will continue to apologize for contributing to yours. Thank you for being great mothers to our children and for the patience between the lines. May God continue to bless you both.

Prologue

This book is for marriages that have lasted throughout the years but honestly don't know how or why they've lasted so long. It is for individuals who have tried their hand at love and marriage but whose marriage unfortunately (or fortunately) ended in divorce.

This book is for those who swore they would never get married again but did—possibly brave enough to have tried a few times and have never explored why they chose to do so.

This book is for those who have been looking for reasons to get married or stay married but have more questions than answers.

If you're reading this book in search of these and other answers, then let me first start by saying don't ask me shit about marriage.

No one has a silver bullet on what makes a marriage successful. Believe it or not, that's a good thing; That may be the best part. Marriage can be defined as a collection of experiences between two people who agreed to figure out life together.

How it SHOULD be done, CAN be done, and HAS been done are all anecdotal perspectives that provide little remedy to marriages if both parties are unwilling to agree on their anecdote. It's a prescriptive way of thinking, but far less pre-scripted than most people think. For example, we can take someone's advice about how to appeal to your spouse to make them respond the way we want - a prescribed idea - but your partner must be willing to follow that same script - or PRE-script - for those ideas to have an effect. No, that's not a word, but like we find in most relationships when situations don't go as planned or expected, we kind of make it up as we go, right?

Are there foundational principles that could help you get to some of these answers? Yes! Are there people with counseling or coaching skills, natural and spiritual wisdom, or various tools that can guide you to a better place with your partner? Absolutely! Is there advice available from someone who has had similar, if not the same, experiences in their relationships that can provide insight into what your next steps could be? Of course!

But what good is advice and counsel from others, principles found in books, or any other research if you never want to confront the real problem?

What if, at the core of your marital discord, the real problem...is you?

Maybe you haven't made the big jump just yet or have recently jumped. If so, you very likely may have the same questions that every married person has had at some point in their relationship: Did I marry the right person? How do I know if this person is the best fit for me? And what makes me so sure?

Marriage can have different connotations based on a person’s demographic, cultural upbringing or status, and beliefs. For some, it’s a means to an end, while for others, it’s a blissful and intentional journey. Most people, however, are somewhere in between when it comes to pre- and post-nuptials. These different views often lead to different experiences and expectations within a marriage.

Should I get married? Have I honestly finished working on myself?

Ignoring cause, effect, and accountabilities in a marriage boils down to divorce; and sometimes divorce, (like shit), just happens. Well, not just happen; shit builds up over time before you must release it. What comes out of you is a result of what you’ve digested. Digest this: If the reasons and factors that led you to decide to get married were not a direct command from God, then you may not have been in your best judgment when you decided to do so. Should you have gotten married? That's a tough question, especially when you want what you want and are determined to do what you had already made up in your mind to do. But the question is even tougher when you’re asking yourself in hindsight years later.

To be clear, I'm not advocating for divorce. If the Lord has told or is telling you to stay and work it out, then, obey the Lord. However, according to global census data, divorces have increased throughout the world in the past 20 years and significantly in recent years. The Maldives, one of the most beautiful places on the planet, had the highest divorce rate in the world between 2020 and 2023. Does this mean because the world is doing it you should too? Not! What it does indicate, however, is that regardless of geography, ethnicity, or culture, we all contend with the joys of marriage and, unfortunately, the heartbreaking pains of divorce.

Yet in the wake of it all, life moves on.

Divorce is an understandable reason to never want to get married again. Ever. Some, however, would suggest though - like riding a bike - the best way to get over a fall is to get up and try it again.

The initial feelings and reasons that led you to say "I Do" the first time all come rushing back again. Mind racing a thousand miles; am I making the right decision…again? Of course, I am! Wait! Did I miss any signs or red flags this time? Did I take enough time in between? Did I wait long enough? Time isn't always the litmus test that determines if you're ready to get married again. Whether ten months or ten years between, getting back on the bike still has fresh memories of the mental, emotional, and sometimes physical scrapes, wounds, and scars of our past.

Arguably, the institution and concepts of marriage are flawed. I mean, how could it not be? We're flawed human beings who "know" what's right and what's best. We have all the answers! And yet it's only in hindsight that we realize either the test was wrong, or we copied from someone else's paper who also didn't have a clue.

What would I do differently? If hindsight is indeed 20/20, I need a magnifying glass or maybe the willingness to let go of what I thought was right. Being stuck isn't so bad, that is unless it's quicksand. From a proper perspective, being stuck should allow me time to reflect. There is divine wisdom and some good practical advice out there about what to do and what not to do in marriage. And whether the goal of those contributors is to sell books, be mass influencers, or Good Samaritans, the truth is (despite misery-loving company) no one wants to see others rotting away in rotten, unproductive, non-progressive, and otherwise unfruitful marriages their entire lives.

Reactions

I consider myself to have a great sense of humor. Not only do I like to laugh but I also like seeing people laugh as well. With all that we deal with and as unfunny as life can be at times, it takes a special person to be able to laugh at situations as well as themselves.

To that end, it's hilarious to see people's expressions when I tell them I'm in my third marriage. I typically would get a range of mixed responses; from morbid concern (as if I told them I was dying) to judgment and avoidance. But nothing is funnier to me, than the slightly tilted head and a face full of utter confusion, followed by "Really?!"

I'm finally at the point where these and other reactions are no longer cues for me to rationalize my decisions. My prior journeys did not work…and that's ok. I'm ok!

In our social media-driven society today, everyone seems eager to share their opinions about love, sex, relationships, marriage, and divorce which results in likes, views, comments, podcasts, and books (wink). It seems more for entertainment value: to see how many of each other's buttons we can push to boost ratings. But in the ashes, are people looking for real answers to some hard questions about where to go in their relationships. When asked about my experiences, I'm usually hesitant to share because who wants to hear relationship advice from someone who has had failed relationships? Well, turns out…there are quite a few considering this is a global epidemic.

Optical Illusion

We create narratives and optics that ultimately end up imprisoning us. Have I worked hard to make something look good for the validation and approval of others, only to later feel stuck in it? Was it all smoke and mirrors? We spend thousands of dollars on a wedding day but not as much as a dollar's investment in the marital relationship itself - before or during. Consequently, we sell fantasy and bliss to convince the audience but secretly harbor discontent and resentment. We have polite and loving personas towards each other in public, but hateful, spiteful, and callous at home. No different than a magician and their assistant working hard to divert the audience's attention away from what's happening behind the curtain. Because if they knew it was all a ruse - a couple of regular people with real problems like everyone else just trying to keep up appearances - they wouldn't buy what's being sold. Image.

But what happens when you're tired of the show? What happens when the chaos isn't worth the fight, and the juice isn't worth the squeeze? At one point in life, I wanted everything to be and look "just right."

What happens when you give up the right to be right and just…be? Be ok with who you are and ok and honest about what you've gone through. Not for the audience. Not for the show, but for you.

And who knows, it might be the insight to help someone else.

I believe there is joy in sharing what you know, but peace in not knowing everything.

Apologies if the title offends…but I’m here now…so Don’t Ask Me Sh#% About Marriage!

Chapter One
Finding My Way

My early views of marriage were shaped by my exposure. If you’re like me, then I believe that we see marriage in the exact ways it appears to us, although there are always exceptions. And in most cases, we will mirror what we have seen. For example, if you’ve had parents and grandparents who have been married for decades, chances are, you may have a long-standing relationship because the longevity of those marriages is something you have seen, believe in, and value. This exposure, attached to your belief and value system, becomes your baseline. But here is where the variances of consideration come in also; whether those parents or grandparents are and have been happily married or miserably surviving; whether those parents or grandparents have experienced any type of abuse or infidelity throughout their marriage; or whether those parents or grandparents have divorced once or multiple times.

Believe it or not, our indirect experience and exposure to other people’s marriages – and especially those close to us – is data we process and behaviors we possibly could mimic in our lives.

My biological parents never married, and most of what I learned about their relationship I didn’t understand until I became an adult.

Relationship…there's a word I'll dig into in a minute because how can you have a marriage without one of those?

Relationships were never topics of discussion when I grew up, at least not in the formal sense. Yes, guys talked about girls and girls talked about guys, but as far back as I could remember, no one ever physically sat me down and said, "Chris, here's what you need to know about…" Well before I can even finish that thought, this was something that ONLY happened between Andy and Opie Griffith on the Andy Griffith Show. Long before social media and before television was in digitized color with five thousand channels and surround sound, there were only three stations - four depending on which direction you moved the wire hanger…maybe five if you put aluminum foil on the tips. But I digress.

This was one of the TV shows I grew up watching in my early years. Andy was the sheriff of this small town and Opie was his son, and every episode he would give Opie nuggets of wisdom that just seemed so simple and lucid. He would make a lesson about girls so plain and understandable. In my mind, all complex conversations would be had this way.

On the contrary, my reality was not that simple. No, it was way denser and much more abstract. What I began to realize was there was no simple way for others to explain what they had not fully comprehended themselves. That would be like explaining the black hole in outer space; people know and have heard about it, but it would take a professional to explain it - and even then, would sound like they were lying. That was the density of hearing someone explain girls to me. And depending on who's explaining would determine what type of lens I was being given to look through. The beauty of relationships is often in the eyes of the beholder.

No one shared any insight on relationships, maybe angles, and schemes on how to get what you wanted from the opposite sex, but nothing as simple as "This is what a boy needs from a girl, and this is what a girl needs from a boy," beyond sex.

That kind of wisdom should have come from one of my parents – like what I saw in those TV shows I grew up on. Whether it was Andy talking with his son, Opie; James Evans, Sr talking with his son JJ on Good Times; or Heathcliff Huxtable talking with his son, Theo, on The Cosby Show. To me, these were the ideal scenarios where fathers would share their thoughts and ideas about the mysteries of women with their sons. Ironically, except for Andy, these TV dads were all happily married, and family, love, and respect were their core focus. I'll share more on that later.

Considering the cycles of life and relationships we all experience, having these talks is crucial to our growth and development. Instead of being intentional in our generational transfer of knowledge and wisdom, it seems the later generations have had to figure it out on their own. Unfortunately, we don't see many examples of appropriate and proper relationship guidance being handed down, taught, or modeled in our culture today generally speaking. Somehow courting a girl and being chivalrous is antiquated and old-fashioned.

I may even be labeled a simp for merely mentioning it. But it bares asking the question: Does anyone still have positive, relevant, credible, and suitable conversations with their young adults about relationships? How do you know when a relationship starts or recognize if you're already in one? Then furthermore, how do you maintain healthy relationships before and during marriage?

Instead, we're left to figure it out on our own. No worries because I heard experience is the best teacher.

I Love Sweets

Growing up, my sensei's were my uncles with cigarettes dancing on their lips as they talked a bunch of shit about what they did and with who. And depending on the uncle, they would either shoo me away when they saw me eavesdropping or keep going down twisted roads of nothingness as far as I was concerned.

The conversations sounded good though. They were hilarious but had no substance or relevance to me. Just sex. I’m not saying sex is overrated, but as a kid it was non-existent.

Then there were my old heads – older guys in my neighborhood that, yet again, talked about sex as if it was only the goal and singular focus for men in life. I vividly recall an older gentleman asking me if I “loved sweets more than p**sy” (he used the word). I was a husky 13-year-old kid with two Debbie Cakes in my hand and a Snickers bar in my pocket at the time, so if I did respond, my answer would have been “Yes, sir, I love sweets.” I embarrassedly smiled and walked away.

I was going through puberty, so of course I knew what they were talking about. The stories they told were no more than imaginative porn to me. But again and again, still no real guidance or relevance. Little did I realize these were seeds being planted. I didn’t hear a single word about what happens between sex or how we’re supposed to interact with women after sex. There was nothing in what they exposed me to that would connect the dots between my first kiss experience and the information and know-how I would later need in a [dramatic pause, hold breath] …relationship.

Here’s an intermediate question, do men and women understand each other enough to advise or otherwise to help navigate someone in relationship matters? Not to mention a young impressionable mind like mine. However, as an adult, I now realize the people I was looking to for guidance and direction didn't have it themselves.

There wasn't one person that talked me through those wonder years. It was all trial and error, mostly influenced by my people and friends who were clueless like me.

From the first kiss to having sex for the first time, to experiencing heartbreak, and then rinse, repeat, and recycle that all quickly followed. What I needed most was the advice and direction for someone who had relationships all figured out. Someone who had the healing balm for every bump and bruise I was encountering. Someone willing to share tribal knowledge to help me avoid the pains and pitfalls I would ultimately get from each relationship. But instead, I was surrounded by people not honest enough to admit they didn't know shit when it came to the opposite sex or relationships. And that's ok! The best response in these circumstances would have required all my "father-figure" greats: the simple gentleness of an Andy Griffith, the thought-provoking and humorous storytelling of a Heathcliff Huxtable, and the straight-no chaser attitude of a James Evans.

The best response would have been from those same uncles or older cousins or even my dad's. Yes, plural because I'm blessed to have two;

my biological, and the one that also helped raise me. I’ll share more about them later, but spoiler alert, them niggas didn’t know shit either. How could I expect them to share from their space?

As it were, my real-world environment consisted of many different role players with varying experiences and viewpoints. Any advances of information were typically in “ask-only-if-necessary” scenarios or disclosed in “as-needed” situations. Those were the lines and those were limits. But what if I don’t know what I don’t know? What if I don’t know what questions to ask in hopes of getting the right or best information? What seemed more befitting was not to ask. You would be looked at as “soft” if you asked because men just figure it out. I believe this may have been the first “don’t ask, don’t tell,” epithet.

Help, I’m Drowning!

Imagine falling into a swimming pool and drowning. As you are trying to breathe, water fills your mouth. You’re beating down in the water, hoping to touch something solid. You can’t swim. Luckily, someone’s there! Inaudibly, you hear them shouting instructions, “Move your arms!” “Kick your feet!” “Hold your breath!” Good advice, but you have no awareness. Who can discern instructions when you’re panicking? As if my brain says to my other body parts, “Cut all that shit out so we can listen to some sound advice." No, our only instinct at this point is to survive.

This may seem like a dramatic comparison, but conversations about relationships were not something men willingly ventured into back then. It was awkward. In retrospect, some of it came from a good place but lacked perception and honesty. Most advice was about the one thing we did understand – sex. I imagine that line may have gotten a chuckle from a few ladies reading this because do men even understand that? Lol. But in truth, this is the one thing, the one lifesaving, water-floatation device that men are willing to throw out in times of crisis. The reason many of us believe sex alone solves our relationship issues is because it's the fruit from the seeds that taught us. Not the only thing, but arguably the most important thing in a relationship.

Outside of barbershop talk, the typical responses from men were avoidance and redirection when it comes to relationships. It wasn't a cultural norm to have an engaging dialogue with the purpose of raising consciousness, educating, or empowering one another to be better in a relationship.

To be honest, I don't even recall hearing the word, "relationship" growing up. "Go-with" or "date" were the phrases I remember. Who taught us how to "go with" someone? Much of what we knew about relationships was passed down from older siblings, (which I didn't have), people in the neighborhood, and our friends who possibly had older siblings. "My brother said, when you get a girl, you do it like this [pumps the air four times]." Of course, I was too young to know it at the time, but it was all miseducation from the blind leading the blind – and the sad reality was neither realized they were blind.

What's Gonna Happen Now?

This was simply our evolution and subliminal rites of passage; how we traversed into so-called maturity. What surprised me though is how common of an experience this was in our culture. I didn't realize how common this was until the movie "The Wood," came out in 1999. It reminded me of those nostalgic moments growing up.

In one of the scenes in the movie, the character Mike finally has sex with his crush, Alicia. He liked her from the first moment he laid eyes on her in middle school. But now as juniors in high school, they found themselves finally having sex for the first time. I say finally because although the movie's title suggests something about their neighborhood, The Wood (short for Englewood, California), it was a flashback of the friendship of three guys and their never-ending quest to get girls.

Back to the scene in focus. Mike and Alicia awkwardly have sex for the first time. It lasted only a few seconds, and although he looks and feels accomplished, she seems unimpressed by the moment. She looks at him and asks, "That's it?" to which he replies, "Yeah, that's it." But then he turns to her and asks, "What's gonna happen now?"

This is where it all begins. For Mike's friends, and many of mine back then, the quest was conquered once sex was done. Like Mike, I wondered what was supposed to happen next.

Interestingly, girls seem born into this world being taught what happens in relationships by way of fairy tales. It's almost as if what is "supposed" to happen in relationships is programmed in them early. There is even a nursery rhyme song that goes, "First comes love, then comes marriage, then comes the baby in the baby carriage." But if you've been paying attention thus far, I haven't mentioned the words love or marriage, and certainly nothing about babies. What's even more interesting is the nursery rhyme fast-forwarded our thoughts as kids from kissing to babies. Not to be crass, but the nursery rhyme I remember was, "Head, head, and more head!" For boys, sex, as our singular obsession through puberty, is what got us here.

Once I began to link the emotions that came with those early discoveries, and the expectations (especially the silent ones), I soon learned why I never heard men growing up talking much about their relationships or their marriages. The truth was, many didn’t know the truth – that is, the truth of what they wanted, (beyond or other than sex), what their women wanted, what their women thought, or how they felt. And like Big Mike, we were feeling accomplished after sex. But unlike Big Mike, we never asked the question “What’s gonna happen now?”

For those who took kissing, sex, and love to the next steps of marriage, I’m sure most would agree that it should have come with an instruction manual and an interpreter instead of those dangling cigarette-lipped uncles we had growing up. But as it were, we were left finding our way through this space as well. And if we’re honest, there were some Deborah Cox moments when you ask yourself how did we get here? If marriage and learning to navigate another person weren’t enough, then adding children and family to the mix can be overwhelming.

Some were fortunate to have church support groups or an elder in the family they could pull aside and ask for advice in the tough places, but a vast majority of us are too prideful to ask for any help. Side note, why do people look at a picture of something that has to be put together using instructions, yet ignore the instructions during assembly?

In many cases, your picture of marriage and relationships dictates how you put it together. If you do not have a picture of what it should look like (or if you had one but just chose to ignore it), you start twisting and wrenching things together with no guidance of the pieces that should fit and not be forced together. And when things started tearing up, we grabbed the instructions only to realize they were in Chinese. So again, "What's gonna happen now?" Whatever we learned or have taught ourselves up to this point in life is the template we use to figure it out.

Either you have the tools to fix what needs to be fixed or we leave it as is. Maybe the template is outdated. Maybe the materials (us) need more refining before they are put together. If we're not careful, we could do enough patchwork to merely drift through our relationships hoping to string together a few good days to outweigh the bad. Til death do us part, right? But this isn't the happily-ever-after you read about as a child. In fact, like a poorly assembled, patched-up bicycle, it could prove to be quite dangerous. Who knew as a kid this was a hidden mystery in the K-I-S-S-I-N-G nursery rhyme: the dangers of Lisa and Timmy sitting in a tree; a tree with no relationship roots and bad fruit for a marriage. (See what I did there)? LOL!

Although there are many nostalgic memories we have of yesterday, the harsh reality, on a larger scale, is not many of us acquired the knowledge, wisdom, or skill to successfully develop and manage relationships. We were finding our way, which unfortunately for some, like me, included a divorce or two. I don't want the tone of my language to in any way suggest nonchalance, because I wouldn't wish those experiences on my worst enemy. But it is something God has allowed me to survive. And what better way to help others than to tell my story?

Chapter Two
Meet Me at The Altar in your White Dress

Why did I see marriage as a last resort?

I settled for marriage. There. I said it. And this is by no means a slight toward my ex-wives. The decision to get married was mine. I wasn't forced, coerced, or drugged, lol. It was my decision, but I can now admit I settled. The word "settled" could be considered cutting or pointed, but according to Dictionary.com it simply means fixed, established; unlikely to change; agreed upon, or decided. Saying, "I settled for marriage," compared to saying, "I decided to get married," could denote a negative connotation depending on the context. When people say they settled for something, it often implies they decided to accept something lesser in value. For example, if someone says, "I settled the case out of court," this typically means the final agreement reached was less than what was asked for. Although the connotation in my opening statement about marriage may seem negative instead of positive, it is actually "both/and" instead of "either/or."

I decided to get married, and the results were less than expected. Marriage was an option I chose at the time to avoid dealing with my ignorance and immaturity. I would have added "in my youth" to that sentence since I first married in my early twenties (twenty-three to be precise), but honestly, I don't think age had much bearing considering I remarried in my thirties. There was possibly some youthful exuberance to blame, and we'll explore that later.

Have you ever "settled" for something? When it seemed right and not-so-right at the same time, or wasn't what you thought it would be when you first decided to do it? Have you ever started a job and on the first day realized the work you were doing wasn't in the job description you applied for? Or maybe it was the atmosphere: something about the place or the people just didn't feel right? You immediately had second thoughts and even contemplated quitting but decided to push through and come back the next day. Whether it was a job, a relationship, or even parenting for the first time, deciding to do something can be a far cry from reality. Think about it.

The thought of being a parent may be exciting until the 2:00 a.m. shrills from the baby pierce through your peaceful slumber for the fifth night in a row. And since you can't quit this job, you settle for what you signed up for - hoping the circumstances will get better. Or in relationships where you get to a point where you think you know enough about your significant other to take your relationship to the next level not knowing what lies beyond the altar of the wedding day. Whether you've been together for a long time or a short while, you convince yourself that you've seen enough of the "job description" to leap.

We Might as Well Do it.

There was a song by an R&B group named Jagged Edge titled "Let's Get Married" which also came out in 1999. This song comes to my mind as the epitome of the phrase "settle for marriage." Whether it's considered creative lyrical writing or a true reflection of a mindset towards marriage, "We ain't getting no younger, we might as well do it," is the line that gets me every time. I did not care for this song at first, however, as a self-proclaimed old-head of the Hip-Hop genre, I came to like the remake featuring Rev Run of the famed rap group Run-DMC. Ironically, it was played at a lot of weddings and receptions, but I wonder how many people paid attention to the words instead of the beat.

I saw and heard this sentiment played out in many relationships and other marriages growing up. I knew what excitement looked like and how people would naturally express their joy over something, but the idea of marriage visualized in some people's faces was the exact opposite. Instead, it suggested a "we've run out of options, and this is our last resort" type of expression - as if they were taking a deep sigh and saying, "Let's just go ahead and get it over with." This countenance recalls the phrase, "Someone is twisting your arm." Why is the thought of marriage deflating for some people? If deciding to get married originates from the thought, "We might as well do it," then why do it at all? This has the negative connotation of "settle" written all over it, and I believe exposes deeper issues.

This is the undertone I get from the song lyrics, but they're sung over a party beat so the mood is drowned out. It didn't dawn on me that real life also plays out the same way. Our true thoughts and feelings, which may be subdued and possibly cautionary, get suppressed by a faux vibe. One day you find yourself questioning your relationship, but then a beat drops, and euphorically, and briefly, you forget about your questions. Those not-so-good feelings do come back and that once enjoyable two-step dance gets old. Instead of reevaluating the relationship, someone decides (the ultimate decision), "Let's [Just] get married." Euphoria and Delusion both sound good over a great beat.

"Hot Damn!"

My family was the epicenter of my earliest recollection and idea of marriage. Although I was too young to process the types of marriages or conditions of their relationships, I do remember they weren't very touchy-feely or overly affectionate towards one another. As I got older and witnessed other couples interact, they all seemed to have that same blueprint or better yet blah print. I don't mean that disrespectfully or disparagingly, but I don't recall seeing the same marital disposition from those on-screen examples in The Cosby Show or Good Times in real life. Sure, these were television shows and characters that were only considered to be make-believe, but what was so inconceivable or made up about being loving, passionate, and affectionate towards your partner? Why wouldn't the interactions of those onscreen couples reflect what I saw in real life? Instead, my real-life examples looked more like "we might as well do it" kind of relationships compared to people who openly and unashamedly displayed their joy and affection for each other. My perspective of this was, coincidentally and primarily, towards the men because of their expressions or lack thereof. Their outward appearances seemed more indifferent and unenthusiastic than affectionate and desirous.

Although we never saw them in their premarital state, I presume my television examples were more than excited to marry their wives based on what I saw in their character relationships. Heathcliff was always affectionate towards his wife, Claire, and the same for James towards his wife, Florida. James would smack Florida's behind as she'd walk away and would often say, "Hot Damn!" She would blushingly smile. As fake as their relationships were, they modeled a very real dimension I was not seeing in my real world. It never crossed my mind then, or even now as I catch an occasional rerun, that either of those couples settled for marriage, but rather settled in marriage.

The Public Displays of Affection (PDA) I had seen from couples, pre- or post-marriage, had subconsciously set a precedent that detached me from being emotionally in tune with my partner or the moment. It was masked as being cool or having swag. However, I eventually realized real-life relationships and the decisions leading to marriage are far more uncomfortable and unnerving. Why, though? Yes, being nervous is common for a bride or groom, but does nervousness outwardly give the appearance of not wanting to be there? I will acknowledge several paths that may lead two people to the sacred altar that may not all look the same, but none of them should be (or appear to be) apathy.

The Only Dumb Question Is the One Not Asked

One of the hardest acceptances for a person to admit is not having their shit together – that is, mentally, emotionally, spiritually, financially, physically, and/or strategically, especially when you believe you do. Let me run that back: It’s hard for a person to admit not having their shit together, especially when they believe they do! I probably could end the book right here, give the benediction, and close the doors of the church, but in the words of one of my favorite Disney movie songs, "We gotta dig a little deeper!"

If marriage is the goal for most people, then we must consider why. Forget the examples, pictures, and images of other marriages for a moment, and dig deeper into "why." What is the reason and motivation to get married? Why is this a goal or the goal? Is it cultural? Is it circumstantial? Is it because of religious reasons? And what I'm about to say may open that proverbial can of worms, but why invite God to the wedding ceremony and not want Him in the marriage? We'll put religion on the shelf for a moment, like we mostly do anyway, and come back to it in a minute. Do people seek validation by getting married? Is marriage a social norm we do because everyone else is doing it?

I can hear my mother asking me, "If your friends are jumping off of a cliff does that mean you're going to jump with them?" This is a legitimate and logical place to break ground because the decision to get married is a critical one, especially if we haven't dedicated the time and attention to exploring the Whys. Sometimes when couples are looking to "progress" their relationships it is rarely asked, or answered honestly, "Why are we getting married?" I emphasized "progress," and made note of this because we'll revisit this perspective later in the book; the reason some people feel they negatively settled for marriage is because their relationship regressed rather than progressed beyond that point. The blissful idea turned into a painful nightmare.

Let me also state that it is not everyone's sole mission in life to be married. Yes, human beings are relational and are designed for interaction and companionship at many different levels. There is social companionship, usually reflected as common friendships are formed. Then there is romantic companionship, which involves levels of intimacy, passion, and commitment. Companionship is a relationship, but that relationship may not necessarily materialize into deep romanticism or other types of love. The general problem is we skip steps. We go from, "Oh you like my shoes?! You want to be my friend?" to "Let's [just] get married," without a clue of the real reasons we ended up there.

There are profound distinctions between companionship and marriage, and they are not interchangeable. One person may choose to have perpetual companions and never get married, and another may enjoy companionship but have the expectation or goal of being married. In either case, knowing WHY will help navigate you and gauge the internal barometers of truth and honesty. There are reasons for every decision. What led you to ask someone to marry you, or on the opposite side, to accept the proposal?

In addition to being relational, human beings are also intentional. Everything we do is with some sort of purpose. Even in cultures where marriages are arranged there is still a choice for those individuals to agree to be married. There may be consequences in those circumstances for not adhering to customary laws or standards, but a decision is still being made to get married. It seems and sounds simple, but some people abdicate their life decisions to others to avoid the responsibilities of their choices. Yes, this is true in certain relationships as well. “We ain't getting no younger we might as well do it,” eludes the real questions, “Do you want to?” “Why or Why not?”

As critical as the choice is to get married, asking “Why” presents the opportunity to explore the reasons. But this juice is only worth the squeeze when it's explored truthfully and honestly. I realize I lacked honesty – first and most importantly with myself. We spend lifetimes masking ourselves because we either don't like what we think everyone sees or are convinced it's not enough. In a close second, I lacked honesty with others. I discovered this was the missing lynchpin that was causing everything I touched to crash and burn relationship-wise. Unknowingly, that dishonesty began a pattern that was crippling any hope of growth and development in my relationships. “Why” did not exist in my lexicon at the time because I felt I already knew my reasons for proposing and proceeding in marriage, and who would ask questions they already knew the answers to? Before my first marriage, I was ill-prepared and underqualified to step into the responsibility of marrying someone. I lacked the mental, emotional, financial, or strategic aptitude to sustain a marriage. What led me to believe I was ready for that magnitude of a decision? I believe it was part-spiritual, but I'll cover that in the next chapter.

Understanding our readiness and "Whys" for marriage helps us better understand our mental and emotional state of being before making that commitment. Being both truthful and authentic are vital components of making that decision. How do you commit to a relationship and not be comfortable in your skin? And if we can't honestly answer why we choose marriage and/or are ready to do so, we probably shouldn't until we know for sure.

According to ChatGPT, Emotional Stability "is the capacity to remain calm and composed, especially during stressful or difficult situations. It involves maintaining a balanced and steady emotional state without excessive mood swings or intensive reactions." This definition is especially true when assessing the "capacity" and "balance" of our lives in committed relationships and marriages.

At 23, I did not have the emotional balance or capacity to conceive what marriage entailed. Neither did I have the foresight to consider or assess what that looked like for a potential wife. The concept of being emotionally stable was non-existent. My moods and thoughts fluctuated with the seasons, and I had not yet begun to understand myself or my cycles enough to provide a stable foundation to build lasting relationships. But I thought marriage would fix that.

Marriage is not a means to an end or a circumstantial solution to issues and problems we are reluctant to deal with before committing to marriage to someone else: whether it’s financial instability, undisciplined restraint from sex with other partners, lack of personal vision and strategy for yourself, or unhealed past traumas or abuse. These are all vital areas that need to be resolved before considering marriage. And that resolution should not be “We might as well do it because I am who I am.” Marriage won't fix you. You can’t fix yourself, especially if you don't acknowledge or accept that you’re broken. Once you commit to the work, heal, and recover, your relationships will be impacted for the better.

Another area rarely considered is strategy. What is your plan for your marriage? Were you aware that a plan was needed? Standing at the altar is not the time to come to that realization. Have you taken time with your spouse or spouse-to-be to dream about tomorrow? What vision do you have for your lives together beyond paying bills, having occasional sex, and accumulating material possessions? Other than cars, clothes, and cash, what direction do you expect your lives to go in, or will it drift into "whatever?" Having a happy and successful marriage requires strategy and planning. It sets an expectation that the two of you can begin actively preparing for. Having a strategy also demonstrates intentionality.

Do you plan to get married is a common question often asked, but what I have rarely, if ever, heard asked is, "What's your plan to stay married?" There's an old saying that goes, "When you fail to plan, you plan to fail." This could not be more true for married couples or those contemplating marriage. I realized by not planning for marriage I had subsequently planned for divorce. And if marriage is the goal, planning for divorce should never be an option. Who joins a sports team planning not to practice and expecting to lose the season? Why join in the first place?

Having a strategy inspires your partner to both GO with you and GROW with you. But if you haven't explored the "Whys," the "How" won't make any sense. Going through my first divorce exposed that I did not have a plan - mainly for myself. Not being solid on my "Whys" impaired my judgment when, and before, I initially got married. It was in hindsight that I discovered not having a plan forfeited my ability to be grounded in my “Whys.” Instead, I drifted into “whatever.” I settled.

Don't Overlook the Obvious

Sometimes we look so hard for answers that are right in front of our faces; like searching for keys that are in our hands or talking with someone on the phone while looking for your phone. It’s embarrassing once you realize it, and maybe even funny if you can laugh at yourself. The most infamous is looking for your eyeglasses while you have them on. What makes these moments classic is when other people are in on the joke, and you are clueless. They’ll have you looking under seat cushions, behind chairs, pulling out the refrigerator, and all the while, they are crying real tears from laughing so hard because they see what you don't see.

These circumstances can be hilariously funny; however, when lives are impacted, being oblivious to an obvious oversight can have serious repercussions. Imagine a bride and groom standing at the altar and everyone in the room can see either one or both don't want to be there. But they are committed to seeing it through, and what follows are days, months, possibly years of unearthing and backtracking steps figuring out how they let “we might as well do it" be the soundtrack of their relationship.

For those contemplating marriage somewhere in the far or near distance, or if you are coming in hot like a 200-yard dash and closing fast, the word for the day is "settle." Make sure you aren't settling for anyone or anything, and most certainly for marriage. Never marry for the sake of being married. If this is your "Why," something is missing, and my guess is that something is right in front of your face that you have not yet resolved. Neither the other person nor the institution of marriage will cure or dissolve instabilities, insecurities, or dysfunctions you may have. None of this will magically disappear on your wedding day. That frog will still be a frog the morning after the kiss. Whatever is not addressed before you get married will certainly intensify afterward. More on this later.

And if you are married and feel you are at a stalemate and "something's gotta give," the next chapter may help lead the way. Instead of settling for the ordinary or mundane, see your relationship and marriage as an intentional union of transcendence, endless possibilities, and a lot of booty-slapping when they walk by. "Hot Damn!"

Chapter Three
Sex, Love, & the Holy Ghost

The crossroads between what I knew, what I wanted, and what I did.

I started the book with my introduction to the conversations about sex as a young teenager. A few years later I gave in to the pressures, and puberty and curiosity took it from there. I fumbled my way through early experiences with intercourse and discovered more than I anticipated. There was something so intrinsic, obsessive, and enslaving in those sexual encounters that I was insensible to; it was like trying to only eat one potato chip and closing the bag. But interestingly, even that analogy depends on what type of chip you get, because what if you mistakenly get a burnt chip as your first one? Or if the chips are stale and outdated? LOL. I digress. Having a bad first sexual experience could scar you for life. I'll continue this later.

I didn't realize at that young age how powerful the act of connecting your body with another person would be. It's obviously what the human bodies were designed and created to do; the male part connects to the female part like two adjoining pieces of a jigsaw puzzle. Simple, right? Wrong. This isn't a chapter on sex education, but if you've experienced it just once in your life, you know sex is far more complex. This "connection" is physical, mental, and spiritual. Sex was much deeper than my

16-year-old self in 1990 could begin to understand, yet we engaged so casually and for some so liberally in these unchartered waters. Sex is addictive.

Speaking of altars and white dresses from the last chapter, this movie line came to mind, "can you wear a white dress young lady?" This is from the movie, The Nutty Professor, during the famous dinner table scene where Eddie Murphy is playing five of the seven characters. Grandma Klump, played by actor Eddie Murphy, is talking with Carla Purdy, played by actress Jada Pinkett-Smith. Grandma Klump very indiscreetly asks Carla if she and Sherman are getting married, and if she could wear a white dress. She then leans in and whispers, "Because Sherman's never had relations." For context, and for those that didn't see the movie, "relations" was a sanitized way of saying "sex," which Sherman, her 35-year-old overweight grandson, had never had.

Almost everyone at that dinner table knew the power and fulfillment from sex, and then Grandma Klump, as if she was remembering her exploits, said to Carla, "When you get a man that's been built up for 35 years, just wanting and wanting… WOO! Might blow 'ya head off." And to top it off, she started singing a jingle, "Sherman's gonna have relations. Sherman's gonna have relations." This by far is one of the funniest movie scenes I have ever seen. But let me get back to my story. Simply talking about "relations" can send your mind all over the place.

The reason I believe sex is so powerful is because God designed and intended it for human beings to not only reproduce but share a Divine connection. Animals also have sex to reproduce, but unlike humans, they were not created in the image and likeness of God; that is, made of three distinctions: the mind, the body, and the spirit. This unique difference among all created beings suggests a greater depth and connection between God and Man. In the Christian faith, The Holy Trinity refers to the Godhead – God the Father, God the Son, and God the Holy Spirit. Understanding this distinction sheds light on our triune nature- our mind, our body, and our spirit, and how each human connects with the other, and more importantly, with God.

Regardless of your religious preferences or whether you acknowledge any at all, one of the greatest mistakes a person can make relating to our sexual connections is to believe that sex is only a physical act. Nothing is further from the truth. Sex is wider and deeper than the physical. It involves the mind as well as the spirit. Whereas the mind envelops our capacity to think, reason, and understand, it is also where feelings and emotions are developed and curated. Nothing in your body will function without first thinking about it – whether consciously or subconsciously.

For example, blinking eyes result from brain signals telling a specific part of your body to do what it was designed to do; and there are many more instances of the power of the mind in the human body. Although this also isn’t a chapter on human anatomy and physiology, I do believe, however, that nothing, especially sex, happens without it first originating in our minds. And because of this fact, the power of the mental connection related to sex must be considered.

I’ve heard an argument that sex for men is only physical. I disagree. The premise for this argument is, that because men are givers and women are receivers, men are more unattached with the physical act of sex and suggests there is no mental connection. There hasn't been a single time in my life that I inadvertently had sex. It always first begins with a thought, then an imagination, followed by a plan. The reason the mind is so powerful is because sex is generated as a thought first. Then the mind envisions it, and from there it plots on it. It could be argued that sex, in most accounts, is premeditated. And for the record, I believe this applies to women as well. I’ve heard women use the phrase, “he can get it” when they see someone they’re immediately attracted to.

The plan and plots may differ between men and women on how they follow through to pursue it, but the ideas and imaginations originate the same. Not only does the mind think about sex before, but obviously during and after. A mental connection is made. The mind is so powerful that years can pass without any thought or contact with a prior sexual partner and the mind can randomly recall an encounter through a nostalgic trigger, a song, a smell, a particular place, and so on. Your mind may be drifting now, lol. Focus. Come back. This is why the mind can't be discounted from the sexual experience.

The last component and likely the most complex of the three, is the spiritual connection that occurs during sex. I do not believe there is a comprehensive way to explain God or His Spirit, nor do I believe it is humanly possible; however, there is something spiritual that happens, transacts, or even transfers during a sexual connection. Some lacking articulation now could describe it as "godly" or "otherworldly." How can I prove this or know it for sure?

A god of Strongholds

Everything in life has its proper place. A chair can be used as decoration in a room, but its purpose is fulfilled once someone sits in it. A house, a bed, a car, or anything you can think of can all be used in ways opposite of their designed intention. But to bring to life and fulfill the purpose for which it was manufactured, it must be used in its proper context. Context matters. And I believe context is connected to the spirit. It is both the illumination and framework that gives substance and life and helps guide us into truth. You can use any of the objects in any way you choose, but when used in the proper context, the truth of why the bed, chair, and car are realized.

Marriage and sex are no different and should be viewed with the same consideration. Biblically speaking, the first mention of sexual intercourse is found in the book of Genesis where in chapter 4 it says, "Adam knew his wife Eve, and she conceived." I also won't turn this chapter into a sermon where I use fancy seminary words like "exegesis," or ask you to talk to your neighbor 18 times, lol. But I do think it is important to establish the framework and context for how both marriage and sex originated in humanity. Ok, I'm sorry. I can't help myself. Instead of a full sermon, here's a quick sermonette:

God created the first Man and Woman, and this is indicative of the first marriage in human history. My first point would be "Stop choosing people that God never made or chose for you!" God put Adam to sleep and when he woke up, he had who he was supposed to be with. My initial problems in relationships and marriage started when I made my choice instead of waiting for God to choose her for me, (or I was still sleep-walking the times I thought He did and had not yet awakened, lol). Lean over and tell your neighbor, "If God didn't give them to you or you're not sure, go back to sleep!"

Next, and to be clear, we don't see anything about Adam and Eve's relationship or anything about sex for that matter until AFTER they disobeyed God, which is also called "The Great Fall." This doesn't mean, and it cannot be assumed, that they were not intimate, affectionate, or relational towards each other from the moment of their creation up to this point. However, their intercourse was only referenced after they were spiritually disconnected from God, and from this point forward in the text, sex is only associated with reproduction – just like the other animals. My second point is "When putting it in becomes a sin" Lean over and tell your neighbor, "There are some things even a condom can't protect you from!"

Starting from my teenage years, what I didn't realize was each sexual encounter I had was outside of its original context. Some of you probably think I'm referring to "marriage" and you are partly correct. The original context of their intercourse was connection: between each other, and with God. Now before you close the book and consider burning it because that sounds blasphemous, allow me to clarify. Consider this. Before their sin, Adam and Eve were intimate with each other and were fulfilled by God (e.g. His essence, His Love, His Spirit). Although the scriptures do not state this explicitly, it can be inferred between

Genesis chapters 2 and 3. One scripture states, "They were naked and not ashamed." As I referenced previously, don't be oblivious to what is obvious. If Adam was swinging, I'm sure Eve was singing, if you know what I mean. eh-ehm [clearing throat to proceed].

Once they sinned, they were spiritually separated from God - creating a void in their intimacy with each other which would remain. And this is where we find ourselves today. We can sexually connect with people, but without His Spirit, there is a void that inevitably causes us to search for fulfillment substitutes. I believe this happens unknowingly. The mind and body still connect, but without the Creator, the third element – the spiritual placeholder is susceptible to the same temptation and influence that led the original Man and Woman to be deceived. The reason sex is so addictive, especially when out of its original context, is because other spiritual influences lead us down paths of self-gratification and indulgence. And before you realize it those sexual impulses are controlled by "a" god instead of the God. And this, ladies and gentlemen, is a stronghold, and it becomes a slippery slope and increasingly powerful as the mind and body want what they want.

Sometimes they agree but most times they don't. Another famous song lyric I recall goes, "My mind is telling me 'No,' but my body, my body's telling me Yes!" And another lyric that says, "If loving you is wrong, I don't wanna be right.” In fairness, this song has a different meaning that we’ll cover in another chapter, but the sentiment is the same, nonetheless. Sex is so addictive that you no longer care about anything other than getting it. Now I understand why the men I grew up around were so laser and hyper-focused on just getting some. It was a stronghold. I can hear a Millennial say, “That thang be thangin!”

And for my last point, said the long-winded preacher, we’ll focus on how we get it right. When we understand how important sex is and how powerful it can be, we also discover what happens when it’s done outside of its original and intimate plan of the Creator. And that plan is marriage. But not just any marriage but specifically to the one God chooses for us. Therefore, if you intend to start your marriage the best way, this suggests that you should first be intentional about asking God whom He has chosen to be your partner. Not be impatient, impulsive, or misguided by lustful desire, but be committed to but wait for His answer regarding who He has chosen for you; and like Adam, just wake up. For the last time, tell your neighbor, “Get’cho ass up!” Lol.

Find Love

The last point in this sermonette is to simply “Find Love.” What’s remarkable about Adam and Eve’s story is we not only have an account that traces back to the origins of humanity, but we also learn of the divine and original intention for their relationship. This allows us to see the good and bad in our relationships and hopefully realize that the discord we may have is possibly connected to the spiritual void that was left in Adam and Eve. Could this be why we sometimes can't discern the conflicts in our relationships or sexual encounters, and even more so why sex doesn't always "fix" things? The void can only be filled by the Spirit of God – the essence and love of God. This is the intimacy and contentment Adam and Eve had in the Garden of Eden before they sinned. But not for humanity to be lost there forever, God's ultimate plan would be to restore humanity, first through the life, death, and resurrection of His Son, Jesus Christ, and for humanity to be filled with His Spirit again.

Here is where my story gets "gooder." I professed my faith as a right-of-passage when I was twelve years old but didn't come into a full knowledge of my faith and confession until I was seventeen – a year AFTER I had become sexually active. This became the nucleus and center of my youthful divergence. I developed an innate fear of God and His Word. Going to church had become my choice and not because I was being made to go by my parents. Learning more about God and His principles were being embedded in me, but satisfying my sexual appetite was my internal tug of war. I knew having sex outside of marriage was wrong, but I had tasted the forbidden fruit, and like the crackhead character played by

Chris Rock in the movie, "New Jack City," said, "It just be calling me, man, it be calling me." I tried resisting, but what I knew (about God) was constantly battling what I wanted "(head, head, and more head" .... sorry, sex). And I often and repeatedly succumbed to the temptation.

At one point, the pull on both sides was so intense, I remember a period I went through where immediately after having sex, I would roll to my knees and cry and pray. It's funny to me now, but those poor girls probably didn't know what the hell was going on. I could imagine them talking to their girlfriends afterward, "Girl, this negro got off me and fell to his knees crying and praying…I don't know if it was that good or that bad!" Lol! I would confess my sins to do what was right by God, but this became my ebb and flow. I later realized the problem; I had introduced my body to a partner (which turned plural) who wasn't intended for me, and that created the void. This void would get ignored because my body and mind were finding pleasure in what I wanted and what I was doing. But what the void exposed was what I had not yet found, "Love."

This love was not the romanticized version I saw in my television heroes, or even in the faux love feelings - which was a disguise of lust whenever I met a new sexual candidate. This "Love" was more like finally finding the light switch after spending hours or even years inside a dark room. This “Love” felt more like relief. I recognized it almost immediately when I saw my wife for the first time. But to be fair, this first time was unlike the other two first times (meeting my now-ex-wives); the prior first encounters were motivated by lustful desire and youthful exuberance. I was barely grown, immature, and thought I knew everything. I got married to my first wife within nine months of meeting her for the first time. That wasn't love. It was what I masked as love to, in my mind, be “right with God.” I had no discipline and was primarily focused on feeding the beast I allowed to run rampant. I thought I knew love, but rather what I felt was the darkness and emptiness of the void. What I later realized was I wouldn't have recognized this unfamiliar love if it had punched me in the face. Then again, this “Love” would never hit.

My decisions and aftermath would lead me from one divorce to another, and a series of devastating yet teachable life lessons, setbacks, and resets. I needed to be put to sleep so that deep internal work and transformation could occur. When I would eventually open my eyes in the dawn of a new day, scars now remind me that I was once wounded, and my flesh was opened. Healing had to take place and with it came a new perspective about “me” I had gained from those past experiences. For the first time, my void was filled and nothing else could take its place. But before the happily-ever-after or even before the work could begin, I had to experience “the night.”

Trigger Warning:

If you have experienced or suffered from domestic violence, the content in this chapter may be triggering. If you are in a domestic violence situation please contact the National Domestic Violence Hotline, 1-800-799-SAFE, for help.

Chapter Four
The Dark Roller Coasters

The pains of divorce can cause irreparable damage.

I always hated the dark as a kid. I suppose most kids feel the same at some point in their childhood. There was something so terrifying about laying in my bed at night alone. I could have had the time of my life playing outside that day without thinking about the nighttime. But it never failed; I would get in bed, exhausted but afraid to sleep. Nightlights didn't help and my mom wouldn't let me sleep with the television on either. It also didn't ease my anxiety knowing she was in the next room over from mine. That dark room seemed to get darker the more I resisted sleep. Some nights were worse than others. There were times my mother had to threaten and damn-near spank me because I blatantly refused to lay in my bed in the dark alone. I don't know if it was because of sounds I heard in my room or if visions of Freddie Kruger, from "A Nightmare on Elm Street" had anything to do with it.

This type of fear is called nyctophobia and it took years for me to overcome. I didn't know there was a name for it. All I know is I was petrified. I could have written a book about it back then titled, "Don't Ask Me Sh%# About the Dark." That may be my next fiction novel. Looking back, I don't recall how or the exact age or moment I overcame that fear; it just happened. I had grown up. I remember, however, a relapsing moment I had as a 34-year-old adult. It was the night I separated from my first wife.

That night was bad. It was eerie. It was dark and I was alone.

We were having another one of our continuous arguments mostly about her suspicions of me cheating, only this one was escalating in slow motion. We were both mad and she pushed every button to provoke me. She was sick and tired of my shit and wanted to fight. The more I denied and resisted, the more enraged she became. The more I tried to ignore her outrage, the worse it got. Years of frustration had come to its final point. Our marital problems stemmed from years of dissatisfaction, distrust, dishonesty, and disrespect. It didn’t matter that I felt justified in what I had done. The “Whys” don't matter after the fact, especially when they get ignored during a relationship.

But on this night, in this fight, I could feel restraint wasting away with each shouting breath of air. A tussle ensued and I remember us sprawled out on the closet floor with me on top of her and my hands around her neck. I was wrong; in that moment and every moment that led us to this point. This was the climax I never expected or wanted. Although, I have never hit a woman, not then, now, or ever, this is the type of altercation where one person is provoking the other to hit them so there is cause to retaliate.

As in prior confrontations, she would yell and scream in my face to "do something about it then," as if to challenge my manhood - which for many men can be triggering. On this night, I pushed her back out of my face as I had done dozens of times before. But this time she hit me in the face and before I knew it, I grabbed her, and in the blink of an eye, we were on the closet floor. And this is when darkness fell.

Let me rewind a bit for context. I would best describe our relationship as a roller coaster; it started in dissatisfaction but was rooted in pride. Deep down, we both knew from the beginning we probably should not have gotten married – at least when we did, considering our age and the time between meeting and getting married. We even joked on a few occasions that we weren't the others' type and saw the initial attraction as a challenge to the other. We married nine months later. I believe pride had a lot to do with pushing our way through the years that followed. Neither of us wanted to throw in the towel because that would look like a failure, and the appearance of having a successful marriage mattered.

On the wedding day, I truly believe we said (and meant) the marital vows, although I don't think we knew what those vows meant. "For richer or for poorer?" "For better or for worse?" It was easier said than done or realized. At the time I had not yet accepted the call to preach but was an aspiring minister. “Aspiring” meaning it was a trajectory my life was on although it wasn't necessarily something I pursued. I did have a passion for God’s Word and convictions about telling others about Him. The problem was my convictions were limited. I’ll cover that later, but I had to insert this as a backdrop because toward the end of that same year, I did accept that call. I was married and now a minister and these two worlds couldn't be further apart. The roller coaster ride had started and there was no getting off.

Imagine seeing the biggest roller coaster at a theme park, and depending on your fears and aversions, you decide - either get in line or keep walking. If you are the thrill-seeking type who finds pleasure in near-death experiences, you can’t wait to get through the turnstiles and onto the ride. However, if you have a fear of heights, you avoid even looking in the direction of the ride. Why bother? It doesn’t make sense or register to even think about getting in a line for that. You avoid these situations at all costs. Some people are somewhere between these two extremes. You are compelled to get in line for the ride, but with each step keep telling yourself how stupid of a decision it was to get in line; yet can’t turn yourself around. You want to get on and are drawn to the fear. Coincidentally, you walk past all the riding restrictions and warnings. Have you ever seen those? If you have heart or health conditions or are pregnant, then you should not ride this ride. Why don't we pay more attention to the warnings and the hazards?

Once you cross that safety line- the line of no return, and sit in the seat, and hear the clicks of the seat belt and safety bars locking in place, there is no going back. Your heart is racing a mile a minute. The ride announcer gives the all-clear signal, and your coaster car gently rolls out of the landing zone area. For a few brief moments, the ride is smooth. But then the next sound is the one that will make you rethink life: it's the sound of your coaster car going up the first incline. This clicking noise is loud enough to wake the dead, and the higher you get the louder the noise is, and once you get to its highest point, you drop.

This roller coaster was a lot like marriage in my eyes. Although I believed I was ready for it, I wasn't. As much as I was drawn to it, I didn't examine it (marriage), me, or the person sitting in the seat next to me. I later found out that having an external view of other married couples was a lot different than my being married. Most of them looked like they were having the time of their life. I saw other people on this ride and wanted to have that same thrilling experience. When I sat in that seat for the first time, I realized the screams and shrills I heard from the other riders weren't all joy. And just like the roller coaster, marriage was a ride I couldn't get off. The anticipation and anxiety grew the higher my coaster car got. I ignored all the warning signs as I ran through the fast lane line to skip the delays and be next to get on. Excited to finally get in the seat, I missed the signs. These were the warnings that suggested I should think twice before proceeding. Think about this, warning signs for a roller coaster are for you to assess your conditions before proceedings, but in relationships, we think of warning signs only as they relate to others. What is the condition of your heart before entering a marriage? Are you well enough to proceed?

I felt I knew my state of being and conditions well enough to enjoy the ride. Besides, I hadn't been on the ride before to know any different. I had passed the point of no return and was secured in my seat and now at the top of my first incline. The first drop took my breath away. This fast-hitting drop was the first realization I did not want nor was I ready to be on this ride. These were the arguments where I first heard the words, "What kind of man are you?" and "I don't know what I married you for. You can't do anything for me!" Then, not even a month after saying "I do," I hear, "Let's get an annulment." I didn't understand it then, but she wanted off this ride too. I was not the person she expected, and I lacked the critical attributes she needed at the time. I was against divorce and knew there would be early hiccups in marriage. This was the adjustment season, like shifting your body in the roller coaster seat after that first drop. Some arguments left me wondering if getting on this marriage coaster was a mistake. But before we could wrap our minds around an exit, the next incline happened. I’ll call this one, “Children.”

Children, both planned and unexpected, are bundles of joy that turn your world around and upside down like the loops and inversions of the best roller coasters. It's exhilarating and terrifying at the same time. Will I be a good parent? Can I provide the best life for them? And once you see their smiles, hear their first words, or take their steps, the joy they bring overshadows any hardships the relationship may have been suffering.

Mine came a few years apart and were two of my greatest life events. Nothing could compare to the moment I became a father although it happened during times, I had second thoughts of being a husband. I did not know how ill-equipped I was to manage marriage and parenthood. That wasn’t the surprise though because most people aren’t. Adjusting to new people and new lives is a part of the “married with children” package, thus the roller coaster. There was even a television show with the same title, although I look nothing like Al Bundy.

We were being thrown backward and forward in that roller coaster seat relentlessly, from one high experience to the next low. This up and down happened every few years - from buying homes or cars to having children. It seemed every high incline was preceded by an accelerating and painful low moment. These were the loops that made my heart beat out of my chest. I didn't know if we were coming or going. One minute, we seemed to be enjoying life and the next we couldn't stand the sight of each other.

Finances initially were the basis of the arguments, and instead of finding ways to edify and encourage me to strive for more of what she needed, her words were piercing and invariably like an overseer's whip to my back. Her words were menacing and sharp. But I disregarded and endured the verbal lashings because I felt I could take it. I had to. I was a man. And since I wasn't raised to be soft, my retorts were stinging as well. Carefully placed and misplaced words can slice deeper than the sharpest knife, but unlike that cut from a knife to the body, the mind does not often heal as quickly, if at all. But most couples have those types of moments, right? Isn't this what married couples do? Break up to make up.

This is the blah-print modeled by many couples. I called it this because a bliss less and unfulfilled schematic of a relationship is not the reason you decide to get married. That kind of roller coaster ride is underwhelming and not even worth the price of admission. After a while it gets old, and when verbal abuse starts, the tongue lashes get deeper. Some couples even take it one or a few steps too far. I believe this is when the roller coaster can get "dark." The mind rarely forgets those moments when things take a turn for the worse. It's like a piece of crystal when it breaks; the damage is irreparable. This may sound dramatic considering how common it is for couples to argue, which most of the time could be minor disagreements. However, when arguments escalate and accelerate and go from bad to worse (name-calling, profanities),, couples must find ways to make up and move on. For me, it wasn't that simple.

Unresolved arguments festered like mold and soon darkness began spreading like stage-4 cancer in our relationship. The venom of bad communication, especially in the heat of arguments, was eating away at our relationship from day one and we never realized how much trauma it was causing. Verbal sparring turned into years of verbal and mental abuse. It exhausted the hope of "for better" and anticipation of "for worse" grew daily. Words can never be unheard. Whether playful or in fits of rage, bad communication can be more damaging and dangerous to a relationship or marriage than loose screws or cracked framing of a roller coaster. You never fully know what's going on in a person's mind: that is, how words affect or possibly trigger unresolved traumas from their past or childhood. The mental state of some people can be extremely fragile disguised by normality. The wrong words exchanged at the wrong time could be catastrophic. People with bad communication in relationships learn to either "go along to get along," that is to suppress their thoughts and feelings for the greater good of the relationship, or like ticking time bombs, they have learned to silently function in the dysfunction. Much like that cracked frame of the roller coaster, you never know the extent of the damage until it's too late. How would you know the impact your words have on your partner unless they tell you or you pay attention to their signs?

For me, "too late" was eleven years later. My response to the dysfunction was finding solace outside our marriage. I cheated and she knew it, and (rightfully so) she was incensed. I had lied about it and denied it and instead of coming clean to make amends, I acted as if her feelings didn't matter. Turning to anyone outside the marriage mentally, emotionally, or physically when you're unhappy in your relationship is never the answer. Cheating in a relationship is never justified. I'll get into more of this later. However, my reasoning was reactionary and poor decision-making. I was beyond repair, and at this point in our marriage and relationship, so was she. We were beyond each other's reach and had enough. I had checked out mentally a few years after we got married and was unfairly coasting for the rest of the years. I was physically present but emotionally and mentally bankrupt. There was a song by the O'Jays that said, "Your body's here with me, but your mind is on the other side of town." I was over the ride but did not want to get off. I was defeated but didn't want to accept defeat. I didn't know how to get off. The excuse I told myself was I was staying for the children, but I stayed because I feared failing publicly. I once heard someone say, "A person who stays in a dead relationship for the sake of their children is like staying in a burning house."

That fateful night, our children were fast asleep on the opposite side of the house. I'm not even sure how they managed to stay asleep through all the commotion that night. It was probably a telling sign that they had become numb to it. That night, laced with insults and profanities, had all come to a head. The roller coaster was going off its rails.

As we lay on the floor with my hands around her neck, I heard her say, "Do it! Do it! You're going to jail!" The very moment she said that I had a haunting out-of-body experience I will never forget. It was as if time had stood still, and I had stepped outside of my body. I could see the entire scene unfolding right in front of me and my hand grip was getting tighter. My mind locked in on her words and the aftermath of what would happen if I went through with what I was doing. Her struggle was decreasing. Darkness was spreading fast. My mind fast-forwarded to what would happen next: me being handcuffed and thrown in a police car as my children screamed through my subconscious. The thought of them suffering the loss of both parents increased my desperation. The next thought was something so unimaginable and horrifying that it had to have come from the pit of hell. I glimpsed taking the life of my entire family that night.

Immediately I was back inside my body as if God had snapped his fingers, but something was different. I let her go and got off the floor. I began collecting a few things from the closet and started taking them outside to my truck, but now in complete silence and a face full of tears. Like a hurricane, chaos was in full effect and swirling around me as I walked through the house into the garage and to the driveway. I noticed the brightest full moon I had ever seen. It seemed extraordinarily close that night, not far off in the distant sky as usual. I remember at that very moment praying and asking God to help me. I pleaded for His strength as I was preparing to leave but most of all I desperately needed his peace. My exact words were,” If I have to live in a box, just give me peace and allow me to take care of my kids.” I wasn't being noble; I was exhausted and empty. My mind conceived an unimaginable thought, and it scared the shit out of me. I needed to remove myself. I needed peace.

From that point, I made a few more trips inside the house to get as much of my clothes as I could carry each time. But those trips weren’t about the clothes. I knew I would never come back to that house or back to her. Those trips back and forth in the house were the hardest knowing the impact this decision would have on my children. With each pass-through, I peeked into their room to watch them sleeping. How were they sleeping through all this chaos? I finally went in and kissed them on their foreheads and left. As I drove away, I had to remind myself I wasn't leaving them, I was leaving the marriage.

This decision would be the darkest valley I had ever faced in my life, and I would have to face it alone. Dissolving a marriage can be worse than death. The person you share a life with not only knows what makes you happy, but they also know the nuances, triggers, and weaknesses that can impair you the most. At this point, I only cared about getting off this ride.

I was reminded in a last-ditch marriage counseling session a few weeks later that according to Malachi chapter 2, God hates divorce. It felt like it was being referenced in a weaponizing type of way; since I was a minister, maybe this scripture would appeal to my spiritual consciousness and produce a change of heart. How can you argue with God's Word? Can you be at peace doing what is described in the Holy Scripture as something God hates? I was. I had no conviction about leaving; the decision to do so was indescribably peaceful. I knew I was not going back to my marriage and that wasn't by any means being disrespectful or disobedient to God's Word. I couldn't go back. Well, I could have been steadfast in a faith that God could change us, and we could be the living testimony and miracle of God's redeeming power. I believe in His capabilities with every fiber of being. "Is there anything too hard for God?" But here's the rub. I didn't want Him to fix it. I knew deep down I shouldn't have been in this marriage in the first place. Was I more disobedient for making the premature decision then, or not going back now? This time, it nearly cost my life and theirs. I chose peace, which to others not knowing the full extent of my circumstances, appeared damning.

Because I was resolved to end the marriage, the narrative was it was all my fault. Someone once said, "It's not what has happened to you in life, but rather the stories you tell yourself." When abuse and domestic violence are present in a relationship, narratives don't matter unless you get help, get healed, and more importantly, get out. We had both been hurtful to each other. I wanted out and she wanted everyone to know I was the sole cause. Besides, what is more damaging to a so-called preacher than his reputation? Truth is, I didn't need help with the bad reputation. She was right and we both were wrong. But the ones impacted the most, and without having any say in the matter, were the children. It was important for them to know I was still their dad, and my leaving had nothing to do with them.

Those were extremely hard times and equally as hard conversations. I am a firm believer that parents should shield their children from the pains of their relationships as much as possible. Not doing so could make them feel as if they must choose sides which I believe can be more harmful. Young children especially are not emotionally mature enough to understand or discern adult situations. Mine wanted to know why I left and were told I abandoned them. I never once shared the full extent of what happened whenever they asked. I was hurt for them as much as they were.

I was in shell shock and trying to function in an extremely dysfunctional way and making it worse. Instead of getting professional help to focus on the healing my body, mind, and spirit desperately needed, I jumped into a new relationship a few months after separating. In my mind, I thought moving on was the cure, but the problem was only I knew the darkness I was running from and trying to avoid. Much like it was when I was a kid, this mess of a circumstance was now my bed in that dark room that I had to lie in. But this time I was determined not to be alone. I had turned the page into another chapter without having finished the previous one.

What do the wounded do when they think they’re healed? Bleed on everything and everyone around them. I was wounded and running with scissors. I hadn't disproved the narrative my children were given about me. No, to the contrary, I validated it as I leaned into another relationship. It appears I had truly abandoned them and their mother for someone else. But this was not the case. I just didn't tell them my side - at least not in any detail. Yet I couldn't explain their pain away. What I gave them was generic and sanitized. "Mommy and Daddy weren't getting along, and it was best for Daddy to leave." "But Dad...Why?"

Have you ever tried explaining adult logic to inquisitive children? You try sticking to the parts you think they can understand, yet their simple questions require more complex answers. Imagine wounded parents, who may not be emotionally stable or aware, explaining to their children the complexities of adult relationships - or any relationship for that matter. There are no complex answers their wiring can handle. If you've ever had to answer the question, "Why can't you get along," it can be as perplexing as if Rodney King asked it himself. Figuratively speaking, fresh wounds can cause you to bleed out, especially if you lack emotional intelligence and proper urgent care. This means you share (possibly overshare) wounded accounts and narratives through warped emotional lenses and unknowingly project your traumas onto others. I guarded my words as carefully as I could whenever they would ask questions. I wanted our time together to be as normal as possible. But what was normal about parents who had been together their entire lives and now for some reason no longer are?

Although I was consistent in my time with them, my "presence" was far from them like the shadowed existence I had with their mother. I was showing up, but it wasn't the same. It was now becoming clear why God hates divorce. The most precious and sacred parts of me had been disconnected. This was the void I feared most. My children…my offspring, were growing apart from me.

Chapter Five
Errors & Omissions

Why did I keep making the same mistakes in marriage?

Figuratively I bled right into the next relationship. Convinced I could self-heal, I pressed forward without getting the urgent and proper care I needed. Like a wounded soldier fresh off the battlefield, I was both badly injured and oblivious to the extent of the damage I suffered. I was taught the best way to get over someone is with someone new. "When I get this feelin, I need," …to go sit my ass down somewhere. What felt like relief was suppression, a distraction from the pain. What made me feel the need to rush from one person to another? Did I need or seek validation through relationships or marriage?

To answer these questions, I'd have to honestly and deeply explore the reason I decided to get married initially. I mentioned knowing your Whys earlier in the book. But this perspective would center on what I believed I needed from being married. In addition to marriage being my guilt-free sex card, I needed to be affirmed, accepted, and acknowledged: affirmation that I chose the right person to marry (again); acceptance in ministry that I made the right decision to get married (again); and acknowledgment from others that I wasn't afraid of starting over. Knowing your why can be misleading depending on the stories you tell yourself.

Timing was another important factor I was not being honest about when it came to making relationship decisions. I wanted to appear as if I had everything under control and quickly moving into another relationship was my way of showing others, I knew what I was doing. I was seeking validation and didn't know it. I was wounded and unhealed, yet in my mind saw another chance at love. But was this love or a rebound? In basketball, rebounds are about being in the right place at the time, or in my case, the wrong place mentally and emotionally.

I met her years before my first marriage during my time in the military, and 15 years later she resurfaced. I was going through my separation, and she showed up just in time. Was this fate or was it a familiar face? I didn't take the time I needed to sort through this rekindled relationship as I should have. Instead, a few months after my divorce was final, we got engaged. Here I was again, running through the fast lane passing those warning signs as if I had something to prove. I repeated the same pattern as before and expected a different result. Say it with me, “Insanity.” What was the rush to make another critical life decision with someone I barely knew?

Ah, I remember. That rationale and timing had to do with her wanting to have a child and her biological clock was ticking. I was so wounded that, not only did I remarry quickly, I considered and conceded to having another child. I call it a concession because I had a surgical procedure done after my second child to prevent it from happening again. I was convinced having more children was a foregone conclusion. But I was needed and wanted to put on the cape to save the day. In the words of Bobby Caldwell, "What You Won't Do for Love." I once asked a close friend if he were in my position would he do the same for his woman and used this song for reference. He said, "I don’t care if it was Bobby Womack, hell nah!" I thought that was funny.

The errors I made before in not counting the cost of marriage had also resurfaced. I was not being honest about how I felt. I did, however, seek therapy and learned something interesting about myself. Affirmations are important to me. I also learned that I was a people pleaser. My ears heard it as a good thing, but my therapist revealed it wasn’t. According to *MedicalNewsToday*, "A "people pleaser" personality means a person feels a strong urge to please others, even at their own expense. They may feel that their wants and needs do not matter or alter their personality around others." And there it was, my "Why."

People pleasers avoid honesty like the plague; honesty with themselves and others. They do so because they fear rejection and either they, or their actions, would not be accepted or acceptable to others, so they acquiesce. I avoided honesty about not being ready for marriage, not once, but twice. Why? Because I feared disappointing the women I had led to believe I was ready for that commitment.

Pause and reflect for a moment. Have you ever had a relationship where you feared expressing your truth or being your authentic self? Why were you fearful? Did your opposite oppose your feelings? Did they know your feelings? Not about what's for dinner or whether they can cook, but did they know the position of your heart in tough matters and decisions? Here's the deeper question, did they know and honor your heart's position? If you can't trust your significant other with your heart in the good and the bad - the things they may like and the things they may loathe, then the vow "For better or for worse" is meaningless.

To feel your wants or needs do not matter is a heavy realization and avoiding honesty is almost a certainty. But here's the plot twist: there are always two sides (my mama would say three sides; yours, theirs, and the truth). LOL. Let's say you are in a relationship where you can be honest about your thoughts, feelings, and desires. Your partner also has the right to be honest about their thoughts, feelings, and desires as well, which may be opposite of yours. You're at an impasse and soon you become at odds with each other unless someone has a change of heart.

In my second marriage, she had just as much right to her honesty about wanting a child as I initially had about not wanting any more. There was no right or wrong, just honesty. I decided and made a great decision to say the least. In the end, another beautiful child was given life. But I was done for real this time. LOL. I'm often asked how conception even happened considering the procedure I had, and many men are shocked to know it did not require a reversal of what was previously done. This was a conscious decision that I readily made. My inhibitions were about the relationship, not the child.

But I still had not dealt with the root of my "Why," and by this time, my bleeding was more profuse. Coincidently, I began having first-time health issues and conditions that I had never experienced before. Internal stressors and traumas were exposing themselves through physical ailments, yet the root of my issues was not physical. Yet again, it was deeper than that.

Heart matters should be handled by a specialist. Just like you wouldn't go to a foot doctor about a headache, you should never consult those who are inexperienced with dealing with heart issues. And the only source fully capable of dealing with heart issues is the One that created it.

Another marriage was imploding for me, but this time without the fireworks. This was the passive-aggressive phase. When a people pleaser internalizes their frustrations and refuse to face their honesty, they act out in other ways. My old habits didn't die, they intensified. I was self-sabotaging. I didn't do drugs, but my pride was intoxicating and suffocating me all at once, simply because I refused to say, "I didn't want this relationship." But not just say it; to be just as resolved as I was when ending the previous marriage. The image of marriage, ministry, and people's perceptions mattered more than being truthful and honest with myself. I had imprisoned myself in other people's perceptions. I'll come back to this later.

I was reaping a harvest of self-destruction and finally hit the bottom. The pit. And now, looking back, I believe God had me exactly where He wanted me. Medically, when you lose a lot of blood your body goes into shock.

"Sir, the doctor will see you now."

Before any major surgery, patients have a pre-op consultation. This is when the surgical procedures are explained, and instructions are given to ensure the patient is aware of what is about to be done. During this time, they are encouraged to ask questions about the procedure.

What questions do you ask when you don’t know what to ask? I’ve thought about this question often in many stages of my life. I always felt I was missing some key information – either from childhood and teenage years or in the varying stages of adulthood. How do you intelligently ask what you cognitively do not know?

I was bleeding out in this last marriage and needed immediate attention. Sex couldn’t fix this and talking about a truth that was deep-seeded and hidden only made it worse. I knew something was wrong, but I didn't know what it was, and you can't fix a problem you don't see. Like a busted pipe beneath a concrete foundation, the hemorrhaging was causing massive internal damage. The next thing I remember was losing consciousness, but I was still awake and aware. I likened this to being sedated by an anesthesiologist before a major surgery. The pain was being subdued but I was cognizant that something in me was changing. The more I sought God for answers about me, it felt like my insides were opened and exposed to the elements. “Feelings” felt different.

Like Adam, I was being worked on, but unlike Adam, my surgery had to save my life because of my self-inflicted trauma. His surgery helped him fulfill his destiny. As I went back and studied this account of creation, I realized Adam never had the chance to ask God questions before his surgery. God determined he needed suitable help and put him to sleep. No discussion. He didn't ask Adam for his opinion, nor did he give him a choice. One day Adam is walking around doing what he was created to do and the next minute he's out cold. He awakens with a deep cut on his side and next to him is something that looks almost like him – except…she's got that "Yummy." If you know you know. From his womb, a woman was produced. I'll come back to this point later also.

Another error I made was not being more focused on my work rather than getting a woman. I'm not implying that men should only worry about getting paid and less about their women but hear me out. Adam was doing what he was created to do - to establish and have dominion over everything that had been created. Today, that could translate to maximizing your potential in whatever work your hands find to do and being centrally focused on your goals. Dominating. This should have been the guidance I received growing up; focus on your purpose instead of the other "P." Tony Montana said in the movie Scarface, "First you get the money. Then you get the power. And then you get…." Let's move on.

Focusing on sex was undoubtedly another error. Please don't misunderstand, sex is a wonderful connection God made, but like anything, can be mishandled and misused. Although I am a man of faith, my addiction was an omitted error. I said earlier I didn't do drugs. I did, however, underestimate what I had gotten myself into. I acted as if sex was not an inherent issue when it clouded my judgment and created strongholds. I was lying to myself by trying to omit and ignore its impacts. Lying by omission is still a lie! This was the self-inflicted consequence of not being more disciplined and self-controlled. I was remarried and facing divorce again.

In chapter two, I made the statement: "It's hard for a person to admit not having their shit together, especially when they believe they do!" One of the worst people to lie to is yourself. I convinced myself that getting married and even staying married in unhealthy and toxic relationships was what God wanted me to do. It may sound far-fetched, but it is a familiar reality for many people. Imagine feeling trapped in abusive, toxic, or otherwise unhealthy relationships, not because the other person physically won't let you go (get out and get help immediately if that's the case), but because of what other people may say God feels about your decision to leave. Whew, that's a mouthful! Let's let that sink in a minute.

Have there been times when people's opinions mattered more than your safety and well-being? Yes, God is a keeper, deliverer, and healer, but does He desire for you to be unsafe? Even if you decided to be with someone you "thought" was the one but turned out to not be? My issue was I enjoyed sex and didn't want to be "shacking up." For those unfamiliar, this is a term used to describe an unwed couple living together in a sexual relationship and is typically condemned from a religious perspective. Marriage doesn't fix a person's circumstance; it exposes it. If you marry because of sex, what you soon realize is it by itself will not sustain your relationship. If he's mean and nasty but gives good love, he will still be mean and nasty when he can't get it up. If she got that yummy but is callous and manipulative, she'll still be that when the cookies are dried up and stale.

I got married the first time to someone I had known for six months. Don't get me wrong, time knowing someone is only relative to the people involved. You can know and date someone for years and the marriage still ends in divorce. Time is important but not always a factor. What matters is learning and observing one another and creating a healthy space where you can be your most honest and authentic self. There was a phrase used years ago in dating called, "meeting someone's 'Representative.'" This refers to people who would only present the best version of themselves during the dating stages. This seems obvious, right? Who would not want to present the best version of themselves to someone you are interested in when you first meet? This phrase coincides with the saying, "You never get a second chance to make a first impression." It makes perfect sense, especially if (being honest with yourself) you know you have some "defects" in your life. Why not hide them for as long as you can, right?

Time for another movie scene. You're at a hole-in-the-wall club waiting for one of your friends, and a few tables over, you notice a woman provocatively flirting with you. She looks pretty good, and the erotic flirting is a turn-on, so you go over and start a conversation. The talking leads to an invitation back to her place. Things are getting hot and heavy and it's about to go down. But then she starts taking off more than her clothes; her eyelashes, contacts, wig, implants, and finally her leg comes off! As you're running to get away, she says, "Don't make me hop after you!" LOL!

Again, this may be a bit dramatic to explain my point, but these "Representatives" are not much different. We display the best versions of ourselves to mask and hide the most vulnerable and fragile parts we don't want anyone else to see until only necessary. Keenan Ivory Wayans' character in this movie realized it the first night, but the frightening reality is many of us don't see this side of a person until we're married, and it applies to both men and women.

The truth is it's scary realizing you may not be accepted for your truths. It's even scarier when you wear masks and forget you have them on. You lose yourself in other people's opinions of who you are or what your relationships should look like, or you conform to your partner's ideas of who you should be. Adam didn't have any say in what Eve looked like and neither did Eve for Adam. They were revealed to one another as their true selves. How do you respond when your significant other reveals who they are?

Life coach and author, Iyanla Vanzant once said of her own life experience after the breakup of a 14-year relationship, she discovered the person didn't love her the way she wanted to be loved. I found her choice of words interesting. She said, "Discovered." As you can see there is no timeframe for the learning and discovery process. When you allow proper time and space, discovery will happen. The "Representative" doesn't last forever. Women typically boast of their intuition, but I believe we all have a level of discernment. The question is whether we ignore it or not. I decided to skip past the representative phase - as I'd hoped they would skip past mine. I was self-aware enough to know I wasn't ready for marriage but had somehow convinced myself that I was. I didn't know myself well enough to have had the discipline, insight, self-awareness, or capacity for marriage. Yet these were errors I made in bad judgment. It wasn't their fault I was incomplete, and it certainly wasn't God's. It was mine. Rushed decisions that caused more harm than good to me and others.

I heard God tell me I was going to marry my first wife, and I don't believe I misheard or misunderstood because she did become my wife. But I also didn't wait for the rest of the information or instructions. Before my second marriage, I did pray and ask God for guidance, but I mistook silence for consent. Word to the wise, if you ask God for guidance and He does not speak…clearly…don't move! You may be asking yourself, "How do I know if God is speaking to me clearly about marriage?" This is an important question that I'll address shortly.

I also believe one of the purposes of my marriages was to be the pathway for our children into this world - and for that, I am eternally grateful. In hindsight, my errors and omissions resulted from my failure to lead with absolute honesty at the onset of those relationships. Instead of leaning in to allow the gaps to be mended, I internalized and shifted blame and broke rule number one.

Chapter 6 – Love Is the Word

"Love shoulda brought your ass home last night."

Relationship boundaries must be established early and revisited often; early because they set the framework for what is and is not acceptable in your relationship; and often because certain relationship dynamics change as you and your partner change over time. Have you ever wondered why some boundaries are initially discussed and not others? Is it assumed the other person understands the unspoken rules? One such rule in every relationship is No Cheating.

Sounds simple enough, but this boundary needs to be thoroughly discussed and clarified. Have you ever considered the same people that teach us about love are often the same ones that teach us about infidelity? I was taught as a young kid that having multiple girlfriends was like a badge of honor to old heads. It seemed cute and innocent then, but these seeds take root and grow into adults who don't manage themselves well. The same can be said for men and women although I wonder if girls were being taught the same lesson as boys. The only difference between the two is that I believe girls are taught to handle their multiplicities more discreetly.

The cycles seem discouragingly clear: jaded adults give jaded life lessons to unsuspecting youth who then get older and reteach those lessons. Same shit, different day. These patterns are recycled for generations. Based on these patterns we learn either how to cheat or get cheated on and for this reason, it should be a boundary discussed early in relationships. I'm not suggesting this is everyone's dilemma, but I do suspect one of the reasons it may not be discussed, and possibly avoided, could be related to past traumatic experiences or lessons learned indirectly from others.

If a person has ever been cheated on, they may or may not be able to articulate their feelings and the boundaries, safeguards, and assurances they need in a relationship to prevent it from happening again. Where there is no clear communication, assumptions are made. Talking about it as a boundary in the early stages of relationships allows both partners to engage in dialogue that should allow for a better understanding of needs, wants, and desires. But again, none of that will matter without real honesty.

What are your sexual appetites or preferences? How do you manage or handle attraction to others? (surely you don't believe you're the finest person they'll ever meet). Why is it that two people can fall in love and not talk about and understand what will keep them in love? If you are serious enough to consider marriage - or continue in marriage - then sharing your heart's pains and fears must be done in full transparency.

You may be asking yourself, "What is there to be addressed or discussed besides just don't do it?!" There is much more beneath the surface of this issue; for one, cheating doesn't just happen, and sometimes the reasons are more complex than we care to explore. This is where my work began, and I needed to get professional help. To understand this as a concept, a person must be willing to detach from the emotional trauma infidelity causes and think about it logically based on facts.

Fact One: All human beings have attractions. Hopefully, you are attracted to the person you are in a relationship with, if not, ball the paper up and start over. "Wait a minute, Chris, that's not fair. What if the attraction has changed or diminished over time?" Visualization is a key, if not a primary factor, in a man's attraction - but it's not the only one. There is a song that says something about a big butt AND a smile 🙂. Women also need visualization and the desire to like/lust over what they see as well. Guys on her social media feed cooking collard greens with their abs out didn't get there by chance.

Beyond the physical, which some consider to be superficial - there are many other types of attractions. Can you be honest with your person if your attraction to them/for them diminishes or has changed? What do you do if it has? Is it possible couples don't have conversations about infidelity boundaries because either or both subconsciously fear how the other will react or respond if there is something about them that the other partner is no longer attracted to?

Fact Two: Options are everywhere! This is an important point that many will miss when trying to understand using emotion; it will also be missed if you arrogantly believe the sun rises and sets on you. One of the most threatening mindsets to have in any relationship is to consider alternatives in other people. If there is someone you'd rather see, talk to, or spend time with (even if just in your mind) other than your person, your relationship is in trouble. I emphasized the word "rather" because when you mentally compare your person to someone else, fantasies and rationales can develop, and once they do, your mind creates moments as if they are or have already happened. Remember that O'Jays song from Chapter 2? "Your body's here with me, but your mind in the other side of town."

And lastly, Fact Three: You can't stop another grown person from cheating. I know I said the last point was important, but this one is most important and can help settle your mind and save you some time. You can't control another human's will and determination, and sometimes you either may not be enough or be too much for your person. This fact is more about self-awareness. Being aware of who you are and who you are not.

The quicker you get to those honest conversations, the quicker you can get to a solution. Having a conversation about cheating intolerances or boundaries doesn't ensure it won't happen. It does, however, set a precedent for open and honest dialogue if interests or attractions wane and how you can mutually and respectfully resolve indifference. The problem is when you love someone incapable of reciprocating what you need. And when you don't get what you need, what do you do? When I wasn't getting what I felt I needed in my relationships, I told someone else about it.

Whenever you seek attention or consolation outside your relationship from a non-professional it can be considered cheating, and yes that is a very thin line. I pondered whether to say "non-professional" because that can be interpreted differently, and I hear $40 can go a long way these days. To be more succinct, I'm referring to professional counseling. Consider this: the moment you share personal and/or intimate details about your relationship with anyone who can't help you, your relationship is at risk. There I go again… "help," meaning in a non-sexual type of way. Let me explain with a flashback.

By now my love for movies and music should be apparent. Eddie Murphy's work as a comedian and actor is a staple in my memory that connects different periods of my life. In his

1987 stand-up comedy movie, Raw, he talked about a hypothetical girlfriend being upset in her relationship with her boyfriend and goes on a vacation with her friends to the Bahamas to clear her mind. On this trip, she meets "Dexter Saint Joc" with whom she confides about the troubles of her relationship back home. Dexter consoles her while walking the beach of this beautiful Caribbean Island as he swings his large manhood like a rope in his hand.

As a young kid sneaking to watch this movie, the Caribbean accent and Bob Marley songs he impersonated cracked me up. I didn't realize at the time how engrossed the audience's laughter was at this punchline – and it wasn't because of the accent or the songs. This was one of those "you aren't old enough to understand" jokes. It still didn't fully resonate until I visited Jamaica for the first time where I saw a few "Dexter Saint Joc" types looking to be "helpful." LOL! "No sir, you cannot help us with our bags," as I pulled my girl closer.

Cheating is often polarized and socialized with the primary focus on men as the perpetrators. The "All men are dogs" slogan has been printed on t-shirts and bumper stickers for decades. But the clear reality is infidelity is pervasive in every societal community and culture. It permeates all genders, races, ethnicities, and creeds. No one gender is more guilty than the other; however, some would argue women are much better at it than men. I probably should have put a disclaimer at the beginning of this chapter as well:

If you have suffered from infidelity, call 1-800-Wit-They-Cheatin-Ass.

I won’t make light of it although it was once said, “Sometimes you have to laugh to keep from crying.” Cheating and being cheated on has devastating and traumatic impacts, which without professional and spiritual intervention is challenging for the heart to fully recover. Although you can search for logic and reason to explain why, there’s never a solid justification for it – even if motivated by revenge. I’ve felt the pain from both sides. The worst gut punch you can ever get is the one you don’t see coming. Neither this book nor this chapter will give any insight or answers to why people cheat or get cheated on other than that shit hurts.

Being in love feels like a superpower. Nothing rivals that feeling. Yet conversely, when the heart is broken from being cheated on can be a deflating and powerless feeling.

Infidelity is one of love's Kryptonite and just as debilitating as Kryptonite was to Superman, cheating can cause traumatic damage. Some people recover from infidelity and can rebuild their relationships and form even tighter bonds with their partners and for others, the infidelity creates a distrust that is hard to overcome. Distrust can manifest in several ways in relationships and its most basic element can be defined as doing anything dishonestly without your partner's knowledge.

I’m not talking about making illicit purchases or sneaking food off their plate when they aren’t looking, but the dishonesty attributed to betrayal, and some would agree there is no greater betrayal than cheating. Cheating is another sharp word, but like love, I believe it has variances and perspectives. I’m not calling this out to diminish the impact, but to dig deeper. Cheating is at the root of most marital discord and divorce, and based on national statistics, is the cause of 88% of divorces. Either there must be degrees and levels to what is considered cheating or that’s a lot of sexing going on; not that I would argue. Whenever I heard the word “cheating” I automatically associated it with sex, as I believe most people do. I later discovered there is more to it than that.

What I will say though is many of our actions are masked by the word “love.” Earlier I talked about the imaginations and fantasies girls are programmed with regarding what love is compared to what boys are taught. Guys have mixed views and feelings about the word “love” and what images come to mind. Those with positive marriage role models may see parents, grandparents, or other couples that exemplify the word “love,” but most of the time when I hear “love” I imagine Halle Berry. No, not the sex symbol many would drool over, but her role as, "Angela" in the movie, Boomerang, where she muffs Eddie in the face and says, "Love?? Love?? What do you think you know about love?"

"Love should've brought'cha ass home last night."

I remember hearing women in the audience of the movie theater cheering when she said that line and it quickly became a household catchphrase. The sentiment is real because the word "love" has been misused so much that it's hard to interpret what a person is expressing. Love could mean, "I like you," or "I like you so much that I want to sleep with you." Then it could also mean, "I like you until…" Those dots are crucial. Fill in the blanks with whatever your "until" is and that's usually where the misuse of "love" is realized.

This moment and phrase from the movie was the impetus behind the movie and so many real-life love tragedies: a player who got played; fell for a girl that genuinely loved him but relapsed one night with the girl who played him, and the next day gets confronted. Eddie Murphy's character, "Marcus" tries to explain his reasoning for his actions and uses the four-letter word - "love." She proceeds to light his ass up and essentially tells him love should have been the motivation for him to come home to her the night before.

She told him, “I'm sick and tired of men using the word love like it's a disease you catch.” News flash Angela, it’s not just men; everyone says it out of context.

While in Jamaica, I heard an expression from the moment I arrived. “Love is the word.” I asked my tour guide why they use the phrase in their greetings, and he told me of the essence and bond of love. It was a spiritual manifestation through the power of one word and that word was bond - like a cement or a glue. Love holds everything together. Dreams, hopes, and desires are all based on this word. Relationships are formed at the expression of this word. And because we can never see inside the heart's intentions, we trust that the expressions are sincere.

There are scientific words that explain the characteristics of love, but love is a word that defies definition. It’s powerful. According to the Bible, “God is love.” That’s unfathomable. I’m not sure our minds can fully comprehend what this means. Everything you believe love to be is an expression of God. But if we rest in that thought for a moment; has someone done something that caused you harm or pain, but they said they did it because they “loved” you? I’m sure you would have a hard time believing God is in that expression of love. Just as our minds can’t connect God, love, and hurt together, neither is it understandable how a person who convincingly says they love someone, yet would knowingly break their lover's heart by cheating.

But why dammit? Why does it happen? Why does a person concede to cheating when they know the harm it causes? Maybe it's not a concession at all. Are we predisposed? Were we shown or indirectly taught how by others? Is it genetic - did we inherit the DNA of cheaters? I don't believe so. What it is though is a decision. It comes down to deciding worth. Now here's where it gets heavy (as if the ground we've covered hasn't been already). When worth is diminished, options are considered.

While you determine your self-worth, the worth of a relationship is determined by the two people investing in it. Like a bank account, deposits make a relationship or marriage grow while withdrawals deplete it. Deposits are the intentional actions that display kindness, attention, affection, respect, honesty, love, and putting your partner's interests above your own. Are you in a relationship with someone who withdraws more than they deposit? Does your partner deposit the right currency or is it counterfeit? Am I suggesting that cheating be the answer? Not! But the behavior must be honestly dissected to get to the root of the cause. Here's a question to ask your partner: "What about me are you dissatisfied with that you may find attractive in someone else?"

As there are many spoken and unspoken reasons why people cheat, it usually comes down to the value of the relationship and whether one or both feel they are not getting what they need from the relationship account. If the honest answer is nothing, this is a diminishing return. Here's what I couldn't admit: at some point in my prior marriages, I did not feel valued - not the way I needed to be. Looking back, this was my honest "why" and why I allowed inappropriate behaviors to progress. I was miserable and didn't have the heart to say so; didn't have the strength to resist; and didn't have the balls to stop the rollercoaster to either make it right or get off.

Chapter 7 – When There’s Nothing Left to Say

“Talk is cheap, and bullshit runs a marathon.”

Healing begins the moment you stop causing more trauma to the wound. Do you remember getting cuts and scrapes growing up? I could hear my mother telling me to stop messing with it [the wound] so it could get better. “*Keep your fingers out of it!*” she’d yell from another room. The more you pick at or bother it, the longer or less likely it will heal properly. The same is true for being in an unsatisfying relationship. It is uncomfortable and can hurt at times. One way we pick at our relationships is through complaining and nagging. To be clear, there is a difference between discussing a grievance or concern and nagging or complaining. If there are grievances or issues in the relationship that have festered and gone unresolved, man or woman up and resolve them, but don’t nag. Complaints without solutions are meaningless rants about nothing. There is a Proverb that says, *“It would be better to live on the corner of a roof than to share a house with a quarrelsome wife.”* This can be gender-neutral because some men can be just as quarrelsome.

We can damage and destroy our relationships by being unable to talk and listen effectively. I would’ve used the word “communicate,” but I believe this involves more than talking and listening. Communication is expression and exploration; its reception and reciprocity; verbal and nonverbal. When couples submit to the process of communication, it can open new levels of connection and commitment. I'll circle back to this in another chapter but remember this phrase: *"Keep the fan ON."*

Communication is like lubrication, which enables all the parts of the relationship to work smoothly together. From running the household and managing the family and children to intimacy and sex (there's a difference), communication only works when both partners are willing and capable of working at it. If one or both are unwilling to talk and listen *to* one another, then it's a wrap - unless God intervenes. But you must also examine capability as well; although we all have one mouth and two ears, we may be incapable of finding a balance between talking and listening.

Do we practice active listening in our relationships, or do we only need to be *heard*? I have encountered people who wouldn't let anyone finish a sentence – as if they were trying to beat the other person to the point of their thought before they could say it. My words didn't have meaning. I grew tired of talking because when expressing thoughts, grievances, or concerns, it felt as though I wasn't being heard.

There were times I felt like the *other* Chris. *"Do you understand the words that are comin' outta my mouth?!"* Effective talking and listening should lead to a better understanding. If there are times you must agree to disagree, then this is when compromise is essential.

What tends to happen over time, especially if one person believes they are the only one compromising in the relationship, is they grow weary of appeasing the other person. This can lead to complacency, which robs relationships of vitality. Complacency is where relationships go to die. I've seen married couples co-exist in communal spaces for decades, essentially living separate lives. How do you honor each other or your marriage in this state? You don't. How do you "communicate when the two of you resolve to just exist with each other with no meaning, purpose, or direction?" From what I've seen and experienced, you don't communicate. You become roommates waiting for the other person to move out or move on.

My answer was to get out…again. I was at a point where I didn't know how to keep saying what I felt I had already said. Going from relationship to relationship can be just as harmful to a person's healing process. The more you try fixing it (picking at it) yourself, the worse it gets or the longer it takes. Here's what I realized in this season of my life: the wound wasn't the relationship(s). The wound was me. I used relationships as the band-aid.

I needed to stop making the wounds worse by rushing into more relationships. Our first instinct after getting cut is to cover it; in fact, we're taught that if the bleeding is profuse, to apply pressure. I sought comfort and solace from other people, and those who claimed they understood the extent of my damage didn't. Repeating cycles and patterns resulted in my self-inflicted wounds. I was harming myself and didn't realize how deep or how bad. These wounds were like deep lacerations to my heart, and it felt like no one cared I was in pain; at least, that's the way it seemed. While applying pressure temporarily stops the bleeding, healing can't begin until the wound is first cleaned, repaired, and sealed.

I also grappled with what was real and what was fake – or rather, *who* was real and *who* was fake. People seemed to like the idea of me, but did they see the real me? Did they know the real me? No one bothered to ask. But why would they if all I presented was the *"I'm good"* façade? I was taught as a kid to shake off the pain and keep going. I only knew to keep going. I was suffering in silence. I was determined not to let anyone know the trauma I was going through but also convinced it didn't matter. Just keep pressing.

This was my masculine idea of perseverance. Taking a closer look at myself, I realized it was a form of internalized self-pity. I've heard it said that you should *"be careful of people that play the victim in problems they create."* This is an acceptable truism. It can also be true, however, that people sometimes need to be rescued from houses they may have irrationally or ignorantly set on fire.

I remember being about ten or eleven and one day pulled a wire from a remote-control car and stuck both ends into a wall outlet. Have you ever heard your teeth click before? I have. I did that to myself and had the nerve to look pitiful when my mama got home from work. Instead of a hug, I got a beating. Sometimes, we don't deserve sympathy but need it anyway. *"Father, forgive [us], for we know not what we do!"*

Then there are times when you have exhausted every effort to make your life, relationship, or marriage better, but it doesn't seem like it's gotten worse. There's a lyric in the song *"Stand"* that goes, *"…you've talked until you've run out of what to say…."* As a preacher, I haven't been at a loss for words many times, but with a second divorce pending at the time, I was tired of trying to explain the inexplicable. Ministry calling aside, this was not the plan I had for my life. I was suffering, but it wasn't *"for righteousness' sake."* My suffering was not due to my stand against sin, injustice, or promoting righteousness. My suffering was due to my choices: to remain in marriages that I knew were over and to not handle my behaviors and responses better.

"You Can't Shit a Shitter!"

This was a phrase my Godfather used to say and my best friend (his son) all the time. He had this uncanny ability to know when we had been somewhere or doing something we had no business doing. Immediately after we'd tell our lie he would look us dead in the eyes, and after taking a puff of his cigarette, say, *"You can't shit a shitter."* We thought that was the most hilarious saying ever, but didn't realize then how much of a truism *this* was as well. The premise behind the phrase is that you can't get over on someone who knows the game and/or has gotten over on others also. The wounds were getting worse because I had been lying to myself. The "Shitter" was still looking back at me in the mirror.

I was convincing other people of a narrative that had a spin on the details, all the while withholding material parts of the story. Have you ever told a half-truth? Guess what? It's a whole lie. The half-truth was, I was effed up and made effed-up decisions and didn't want anyone to know. I felt I was an embarrassment to the ministry calling on my life - which deserves (demands) a moral standard be upheld in the character of being self-controlled, tempered, and long-suffering among many other attributes.

The whole truth was that my private walk did not match my public faith. My quasi-attempts of repentance were to dissolve one relationship and move on to the next. These were the "limited convictions" I referenced in an earlier chapter - the strong views, opinions, or stances against some lifestyles or behaviors, but more forgiving to others. These are typically where we may also be the offenders or partakers. The whole truth was that although I was apologetic and remorseful, I didn't deal with my lacerated heart.

To fully repent in heart, body, mind, and spirit would mean I'd have to finally stop repeating cycles and stop talking. I would have to listen and submit to my process. My wound needed to be cleaned. *"Hezekiah!" "No music....' Won't He make you clean…inside!'"* You'd have to be a church kid to get that one, lol.

It would be almost impossible to recover from two divorces and move on again as if nothing had ever happened. I was clear this time through about one thing: I was never getting married again. Two was enough…no mas! I began shutting up and shutting down at the same time. I desperately needed God's Divine help because my way was not working. I couldn't get out of my way. I didn't have the words to explain it away. The pain I had caused and the pain I was in was far beyond what my words could express.

Now in my mid-forties, I had come to the realization I couldn't outrun my problems, and I couldn't outrun myself. But most importantly, I couldn't outrun God.

As I sat in a therapy session one day, God showed up. My therapist didn't begin radiating with a glow. I didn't see a vision appear like the one Malcolm X had of Elijah Muhammad. I did, however, have the same type of experience as the scriptures reference of the prophet Elijah. The still, small voice.

My therapist asked me a simple question: *"Who are you hiding from?"* I heard his words, but it wasn't his voice. This voice shook my insides as I looked at him with a puzzled look. I heard the question, but I also recognized the voice. The voice was gentle and tender. It wasn't condemning but was affirming and reassuring. This question was not from a chapter or verse of the Bible, but it was unmistakably *His Word*. My initial answer to the man sitting across from me was, "I don't know." But I did know. I just didn't want to say or admit it out loud. I was hiding from the opinions, judgments, and disapprovals of people.

I was caught off guard, yet the tone in the Voice was calming. God asked Adam "why" he was hiding in the Garden of Eden. I learned that God speaking in this moment indicated to Adam His presence was near. Why is it that we sense God's presence right after we've done something wrong? Adam heard God's voice, and because of his disobedient decision, he experienced fear for the first time.

Please allow me to speak to your heart at this moment. If God has revealed himself to you in some way, and it's after something you may have done wrong, it's not to bring you harm. He is loving, forgiving, and redeeming and has shown you His presence to remind you that you belong to Him. Don't allow self-condemnation or people's judgment to keep you from acknowledging His presence.

I don't believe the voice Adam heard and the one I heard were much different. When this story was read to me as a child, the narrator imitated God's voice in a harsh and scolding tone. Condescending. Now that I'm older, I don't believe it was a tone of condemnation. Why would God, who knows every choice and decision we make before we make them, condemn you for what He knows you'll do?

Discerning tone in this context may seem unnecessary, but if you've never been scolded for doing something bad, you already know the impact that can have on the rest of your life. For the detractors, I'm not implying there should be no guilt when we do wrong. Humans seem to want people to stay under the clouds of guilt and condemnation. This becomes a method of control rather than helping each other be better and get better. We've fashioned God to take on our mannerisms and disposition instead of the opposite.

I've contended with this most of my life.

People are more disowning and unforgiving than God. It was instilled in me that God was angered intolerable of bad and disobedient behavior. I later realized it was people imitating God for their selfish gain. That voice I heard that day in those five words was no imitation. Those words, *"Who are you hiding from?"* spoke volumes and were both my question AND my answer.

Chapter 8 – Ethos and XLV

"Fix your crown, King, we need the Blueprint."

My turning point had arrived, and I needed to take inventory of where I was mentally, emotionally, and spiritually and move forward. I made apologies where I could and was mindful to not allow my traumas, other people, or their traumas to imprison me again. This is when *I'm sorry* isn't enough for some people, and they want you to suffer until they feel better. If you've ever broken free from this type of manipulation, then don't ever go back.

This was also the time I felt the aftershock from both divorces. No one talks about the realities of post-divorce stressors. Losses that impact your children, family, finances, and lifestyle, prove to be as unstable and unpredictable as the ground after an earthquake. This may sound like a slogan from a rehabilitation center, but recovery can only happen one day at a time. Both the good and bad of relationships take their toll.

One minute you are unsure if you've made the right decision, and the next, you're discovering what it means to be single again. You try to find ways to co-parent without re-triggering your trauma or theirs, if co-parenting is even possible. You go from a two-income household to one and feel the pain of starting over. The curiosities of family and friends are also factors. Imagine having to retell the story of "what happened?" dozens of times and then be subjected to the "What y'all need to do is..." opinions. It's exhausting.

This could be the reason why some couples resolve to stick it out. Well, this and Johnnie Taylor. Johnnie Taylor had a song that said, *"It's cheaper to keep her,"* considering most divorces incur significant financial impact and loss, many men believe they are better off staying together. If you decide to stay together, I will be the first to lift both your hands in celebration with you; make sure it's not for reasons in your relationship you don't want to face.

The fears of the financial impact, the other person moving on to someone else, opinions of others, and fears of being alone or of starting over are a few reasons both or either person may resolve to remain in discontent relationships. The most disheartening reason I've heard of is the person suffering abuse and living in fear of more physical or psychological abuse or manipulation. This is when a person has a mental hold on their partner and can manipulate them to stay in the relationship. Leaving a relationship is never easy, but it may be necessary, and in cases of abuse and manipulation, your life may depend on it. Get the help needed to do what's best.

Both divorces left me in raw places.

Although I never regretted those decisions, I can’t lie, the painful aftershocks, especially those that affected the kids, made me second-guess a few times. I knew going back wasn’t the answer, but I also understood how couples with children make decisions they believe are in their best interest to stay together. Some believe that having both parents under the same roof when their relationship ends can make the children think that the family is intact.

The question I had to ask myself was, “What’s the point of being present if the parents and kids know it’s toxic and unhealthy?” Since we are all wired with different family ideals and sensibilities, these answers will certainly vary. As previously mentioned, if your reference to family and relationships were having both parents at home, aware they had problems and at times (or most times) didn’t like or seem to love each other, your value may be placed on both parents being in the same home no matter what. If your upbringing and views were different, then it’s likely your decisions will mirror your values in these circumstances.

Some parents try to hide their dysfunction while others can’t. Either way, in my opinion, children at a certain age of awareness are just that…aware. They know when parents aren't happy and are better off apart than together. Once I realized that either decision would not avoid the need to parent them through painful and traumatic shifts and countless questions, I needed to become the healthiest and happiest version of myself for them. The aftershock of multiple divorces impacted my children and finances, and now it was time to not only pray for my life to get better, but it was time to make changes. Faith without works is dead.

I now needed to focus on refinement. Those preconceived fantasies of what marriage would be like I referenced at the beginning of this book were over. I had gone through humbling experiences but felt as if I had broken through my cocoon. I could now sit with my therapist and be completely honest about where I was and why I was there. I now had a post-married mindset, which was mostly cemented in never getting married again. Not only was I saying it, but I meant it. I stood on it and in it as solidly as if I were pouring cement around my feet.

My therapist cautioned me not to be so absolute in that thinking and that it was possibly linked to my post-traumatic stress. Maybe they saw something about my wiring that I was not yet willing to concede. I'll come back to this. We tend to make rash and emotional decisions after stressful and traumatic experiences, and some experiences are meant to refine us instead of running us away. Have you done or sworn not to do something based on the result of a previous experience only to find yourself in a similar experience later?

I believe these are cycles that we can only overcome once the lessons are learned. My lesson was to not rush into any more marriages. But I swung the pendulum just as fast in the opposite direction, never wanting to experience it again. Wherever you find yourself on the relationship spectrum, make sure it's because you've examined yourself carefully and honestly and are making a sound decision that is both spiritually and practically guided.

One day, I made a social media post about self-encouragement and pushing through the pains of yesterday. I read a comment that said, *"Fix your crown, King, you good."* That phrase stuck with me, but not for the obvious encouraging reasons. I was done making it look "all good" when it wasn't. This was the process. *My* process. And I now, more than ever, needed to be ok not being ok for a minute. What do you do when you're 45 years old and divorced twice? Not that! Well…*AFTER* that! LOL! Yep, you guessed it. You get a tattoo!

My journey continued. I know I'm late to this party for those who have been getting inked since they could walk. I had those "limited convictions" I mentioned earlier in the book. This is where I realized I was spiritually opposed to some behaviors compared to others. For example, I had issues with tattoos because someone once pointed out in scripture that they were a sin, yet I made excuses about cheating. I discovered I wasn't alone. I later realized it's embedded in human psychology to create a rationale for behaviors we accept and castigate those we hate or are uncomfortable with.

As you examine yourself, have there been areas you felt strongly against but expected leniency when it involved you? This is not to make light of any transgression, but the Book says that if we transgress against one part of the law, we have transgressed against the whole law. This is for those who believe their sins may be of lesser significance or consequence than someone else's. Thank God for His amazing and saving grace!

After experiencing a second divorce, I wanted a tattoo. I would now be a divorced AND tatted preacher. As trivial as this may seem, it was a huge step and bold declaration of finally accepting me despite how anyone else may feel. The tattoo was of a scowling lion bearing a tilted crown with the Roman letters "XLV" inscribed. I chose not to fix my crown. Instead, this art expression would represent how I saw myself – a flawed king with imperfections but a king, nonetheless.

Up to this point, I have not shed much light on my spiritual character – the title and content of the book may be an outright disqualifier for some. Some in the Christian community or other faith-based beliefs may argue that using foul language indicates a lack of character and is unnecessary. But which is more offensive, saying "shit" or doing shitty things hoping no one sees or knows about it? One of my brothers used to say, *"There is no easy way to do hard shit."* I chose not to sanitize my words because there are times when selective and censored language doesn't fit the moment.

One of my favorite Gospel singers once said Christians should uphold a different standard from the world. No argument from me there. They went on to say that even late at night on your way to the bathroom and you happen to stomp your toe, a Christian should not curse. *Sheeeeeeeit.* LOL! Don't strike me down, Lord! (Did y'all say that as kids, too?) I'm not making light of using offensive language, but whether you agree or not, there may be times when there are some people (including the hypocritical religious) who don't curse yet live nasty lives.

Character isn't only about choosing the appropriate words; it's about living what you believe. At this juncture in my life, I began re-affirming mine. According to Merriam-Webster, "character" is defined as *"attributes or features that make up and distinguish an individual."* But it also means *"moral excellence and firmness."* How would excellence and firmness be characterized considering what I had gone through? Accountability. Experiencing adversity does not indicate a lack of character – although some could argue it involves making better choices to avoid adverse situations – but the real character is developed through adversity.

Are you quick to acknowledge and correct offenses? Does *"I'm sorry"* result in a change of behavior? Here's a big one that hit me hard: does your private behavior match what you display in public? This may seem inherently simple, but it is a principle that includes every red-blooded human being. Private behavior can be in our minds and hearts and not only the four walls of our homes. Doing my work required acknowledging where my marriages failed and where I failed my marriages.

I was pastoring and secretly harboring illicit thoughts and behaviors, and God said, *"Enough."* Although I repented, I still had to face the consequences of the seeds I had sown. My darkness had come to light - even if not obvious to everyone - the illuminance was for me. Embarrassingly, in the aftermath of another failed marriage, this too was heavily criticized and frowned upon in the faith community. Up to this point, my spiritual character had become a façade, but unintentionally. It was not my intent to pose or to appear as if I was an exemplary standard or representation of a Christian or community leader.

I was purposeful, however, to only show others what I believed they needed to see – this was before 'posing for the gram' became a thing. I was taught to *"keep people out of your business."* The difficulties surfaced when the life I preached about and wanted to live publicly did not match the private and internal turmoil I faced for nearly 20 years. During my first divorce, I recall one of my spiritual leaders mentioning that no one would have ever known what we were going through from the outside looking in. Some in the faith community had a hard time accepting (and even I did for a period) that God had covered me through my most vulnerable time.

In Genesis, there is an account of Noah one day being so drunk after the flood that he passed out in his tent naked. In my Bernie Mac voice, *"Bucka-Necc'ed!"* One of his sons came into his tent and saw him naked, then ran out laughing to tell his brothers. The other two sons walked backward into Noah's tent with a sheet stretched between them and covered him up. This demonstrated compassion.

I believe God allowed me to be covered in my time of failing and nakedness so I would be able to do the same for someone else. I know what failing feels like. I know what failing out loud feels like. But I can also say I know what gracefully covering others feels like as well. Covering someone does not mean you support their actions or what they feel, but rather, you empathetically support and conceal them when they need it most until they can get it right.

A friend going through a tough time in his marriage once asked how I knew it was time for a divorce. My almost knee-jerk response was, *"If you're asking the question, you're not there, and you should go back and make it right with your wife."* I was telling him to go back and cover her. I didn't ask for, nor did I want, the details of why he had asked the question. Based on the question I knew he was asking, *"How do I make this rollercoaster stop?!"* My heart and prayer for them was that they figure out whatever the issues were and fix them.

I knew what it felt like to be unfulfilled in a relationship with no end in sight, but I also recognized hope when I saw it. Would it be hypocritical for me to encourage someone to stick it out in their marriage when mine failed? Not. It was the opposite. My advice and answer to him is the same for anyone else asking that question - man or woman: *"Go back and make it right!"* I am thankful that he did go back and make amends, and I saw their marriage and love for one another go to another level.

Although the Bible specifies adultery as an "acceptable" ground for divorce, I believe there are others - although not mentioned specifically in scripture. For example, abuse and abandonment are not listed as reasons but are legitimate. I realize divorce has been a debated topic throughout human civilization, and although it may not be ideal for some, it may be necessary for others - especially when life, state of mind, and well-being are at stake. This is also why getting help, counseling, and spiritual guidance are all critical to gaining insights into the next steps in suffering relationships.

Another painful reality of going through divorce once is the possibility of it happening again - partly because you know some of what to expect. Divorce teaches you how to escape. I truly believe some people are made for one another, and divorce should never be a considerable option. However, when relationships take traumatic turns, divorce is not an option for consideration - it is the only solution. No questions asked or advice needed. This is why I knew my friend wasn't *"there"* when he asked how I knew it was time for a divorce. People don't ask for advice when their minds are made up. This is usually because they have spent time seeking advice and trying to make their relationships better. The fact that he inquired told me there was a possibility their relationship could and would get better. There was a glimmer of hope, and I could see she was made for him.

Having the *right* partner can help bring life back into proper perspective. And yes, I know, *"right"* can be relative, so I'll clarify: for men, the right partner is someone who can hear, discern, and respect his voice; for women, the right partner is someone who can handle her heart with love and tenderness. In its most basic forms, men need respect, and women need love. But aside from *having* the right person, you must likewise *be* the right person. Being right for one another means you are willing to sacrifice ego, selfishness, and pride for the other person's betterment. There is no better commitment to moral excellence and firmness than to stand ten toes down for each other in tough times.

There is hope for marriage and relationships when two people know they are right for one another and choose to cover each other while doing the work it takes to MAKE IT RIGHT. Ask yourselves, do you want what's best for one another, and if so, how do you show it? Can you cover one another's flaws or weaknesses, or do you laugh at their nakedness and want others to see? Are you compassionate towards each other or in competition against one another?

Although I was adamant that I would never get married again after the second divorce, the cement I had poured on this statement, which I was standing ten toes on, was still wet. I should've known better because I had learned enough lessons to know you should ***never*** say never. Life and the God of our lives will, at times, cause you to revisit decisions that may not align with His plan for your life. During this season of repair, recovery, and rehabilitation, I began thinking about my design and my desires.

I had always esteemed marriage as the foundational component of family and felt early in life that being a husband was my rightful place. However, the pain from failed experiences soured my desire to consider marrying again. Truthfully, I was not prepared to be a husband the first time, nor did I understand the time needed to heal before considering marrying again the second time. At the heart of my internal dilemma was the conflict between what I was made to be and the scars that reminded me of those experiences. I had now learned what it meant to be a husband and the importance of having time to heal.

At 45, although I no longer wanted to be married, I knew I was wired to be a husband. I had developed the attributes and instincts to provide, protect, and cover those I cared about to my best abilities. These characteristics by themselves do not make a man a husband. But by every definition, a husband demonstrates these offerings *and* is married to a wife. I knew I was made to function within this capacity because it wasn't something I could shake. But I was a two-time divorcee, and any consideration of a long-term relationship had to be marriage. This is where the strange stares and confused looks come in because why would the thought of being married again ever be a consideration? This was my epiphany at 45. I discovered that the best of who I was created to be, would be realized in the *right and married* relationship.

Some with similar experiences with relationships, marriage, and divorce swore to never marry again and have either settled into a better mental space as a life partner or happily single. As I said earlier, it is NOT everyone's desire to get married, and again I say, this must be openly discussed and accepted with your person in the foundations of your relationships.

A deeper look into my soul revealed my issue wasn't with my wiring and desire to be fulfilled as a husband but with compatibility. I was always told "Happy Wife - Happy Life" and advised to fulfill my wife's needs, wants, and desires, but I was never informed how to be fulfilled as a husband. I never assessed if she had what I needed beyond sex. As simple as men are, sex is not a cure-all. I had rushed relationships into intimacy, bypassing full compatibility checks. Write this down: *"Sex is meaningless if the rest of you does not fit the other person."* Finding the right fit requires work. It's the investigation, humility, prayer, and accountability we tend to overlook early in relationships. Women seemed to be more astute at doing this than men. Up until a recent trend in two-way compatibility checks, men had typically and only relied on the genital fitment test. But it's in hindsight that we (both men and women) realize this superficial lack of focus resulted in experiences of pain, frustration, and anguish.

Prince Hakeem said in *Coming to America, "I want a woman who can arouse my intellect as well as my loins,"* while his father, "the King," was only interested in whether Hakeem had sex with his bathers. (Did you read that last line like it was said in the movie?) LOL! This movie was about finding love as well as compatibility, and he went across the world to find his queen in Queens. Instead of spinning a globe of randomness, hoping to land in a fated destination of love, try some intentionality.

If you were to create a list of ideal traits compared to your partner, what would be missing? Here's the twist: these traits should not be superficial: *"I wanna girl with extensions in her hair, bamboo earrings, at least two pair."* Instead, they should be more character-based, like values, morals, beliefs, likes, and dislikes. You may discover your partner may not check every box, and that's ok. You like some parts of them but not others. That's both reasonable and, to some degree, expected. Guess what? You likely don't check all their boxes either. Ego-check-1-2.

The goal of this exercise is not for the person with these ideal traits to be identical with yours, but rather a compatible match; their ying to your yang; their fire to your ice. It's almost zen-like in that you "know when you know" type of connection. The perfect fit provides balance. I was now beginning to understand that if I were to ever marry again, the "right" person had to fit me perfectly. My design matrix or “blueprint” demanded it, and there was no room for compromise this time.

The blueprint is a mapping of our mental and emotional design. On the surface, it's how we understand and communicate our needs, particularly in relationships or potential relationships. These are the intricate details of who you are, your likes and dislikes, your vulnerabilities, and all the data you have collected from every relationship. Those that ended well and especially those that did not all have notes stored in the schematic of your blueprint.

Blueprints are often used as guides when meeting people. The problem is the blueprint also becomes your playbook, and encountering the wrong type of “character” can make you susceptible to manipulation. How many of us can admit there may have been times we’ve given the blueprint away too early? Don’t forget, that hurt people are capable of hurting people. Although you may be sincere in developing or maintaining relationships, anyone with bad intentions now has your blueprint and can potentially cause even more trauma.

For example, you meet someone who checks a few of the items on the checklist, and by the first or second date, you start telling them everything that happened to you in past relationships: what the last person did and how it made you feel. It may seem innocent to have these types of discussions upfront. The rationale may also be in the interest of transparency and not wasting time, but little do you realize you have given this information to the person's "Representative." They now have a map of your thoughts and emotions and can put on their cape and save the day! *"Say whaaat…she did what to you?"* Or *"He did what? Nooo…" "Hold up, I'll be right back!" [comes out of the restroom with red tights on]"* Here *I come to save the Daaay!"*

Chapter 9 – Black Superman

Believe in the strength you've been given and avoid what makes you weak.

As a people-pleaser, I believed my superpower was to make everyone's world better. As I mentioned before, not only was this unrealistic, but it was also unsustainable. My "representative" would get the blueprint, and from there, *"Up-up and away we go!"* The blueprint gave me insight into what someone needed and how I could best show up to satisfy those needs. But my handsome representative often failed to mention and disclose that I, too, needed something in return. If I didn't get what I needed, and if what I needed was not reciprocated, then my super abilities became limited and conditional, if not completely null and void.

Superpowers are the ability to do the extraordinary feats that make you different. They allow a person to "show up" in their distinct uniqueness. But imagine what it would feel like or mean to no longer be considered "super" in your relationship. The way you would take all the groceries in from the car - 50 bags at once no longer impresses; or making sure all the smoke detectors had fresh batteries and wouldn't constantly beep for two years; or being the caring, attentive, and listening ear, they fell in love with doesn't have the same appeal. Or what if that "smack-it-up, flip-it, rub-it down, Oh Nooo…no longer works? (Oh Nooo, for real). What used to solve the problem or save the day no longer does.

Have you ever been in a budding relationship or marriage that by all accounts was going great, and out of the blue, it began to fizzle? Most times, the fizzle is indicative of those unique abilities being taken for granted. One or both partners are no longer "Wowed" by the other. And this reaction is beyond mere feeling. The person producing their ability may not be getting what they need in return, or the other person may no longer be satisfied. Herein lies a conflict so big it unroots 100% of the 88% percent of marriages that end in divorce. Someone isn't happy in the relationship. No surprise there. But why?

For those who grew up watching and idolizing superheroes like I did, Superman was the first comic book hero I can remember. Others followed, but he was the first. Side note: Argue with someone else, but the '80s had the best after-school and Saturday morning cartoons ever! Period…end of discussion…back to the subject.

Despite whomever your favorite character was, I imagine you, like me, were in awe of their superpowers. No matter the situation they faced, they seemed to have the right type of power needed to overcome any adversity. At the end of each episode, everything they needed to come out was due to a power they possessed. Remember this for later: ***Greater is He that is within me!***

Did you ever wonder why they were compelled to save the day? Was it because of a deep sense of morality, justice, or equality? Was it the satisfaction of saving those who couldn't save themselves? Or were they secretly satisfying a need to be needed? Was it esteem they were seeking? If so, why would those with superpowers need to be esteemed by people without powers? The plots of these storylines thickened every week. Whatever the hero's motivation, in the end, they always showed up.

I didn't wear a cape mask or carry a sword, but I knew how to show up for others. The problem I faced in relationships was not knowing why I felt the need to save the day. Well, duh, I had the power, abilities, and blueprint to be what someone else needed me to be. I learned not everyone wanted or needed to be rescued...by me. I learned that my gifts, skills, and abilities, although unique to me, were not all sufficient for others. My superpowers could fix some problems but were not a perfect fit for everyone's needs.

Everyone has powers. Even Superman had his friends in the Justice League. They all knew their special strengths, which united them for a cause. I started realizing my relationships were not about the powers themselves but about compatibility and what was the best fit for me and them. From friendships to romantic relationships, the real blueprint is finding your match. This was also very much rooted in my spiritual design, as well as my relationship with God.

God began showing me where I needed more of His Spirit to finally overcome the torments I suffered. Therapy was a great tool and resource for me during my healing process, but I needed to consult with the One who created and equipped me with these powers. In becoming the best versions of ourselves, the created must reconcile with the Creator and coincide with His power. Only God can solve the mysteries of our lives and give clarity to marriage and relationships. Why? Because God also created the people in the relationships, and to understand your powers, you must submit to the super. *"All to Jesus, I Surrender."*

I needed to know why, despite all my powers and abilities, I was unable to break free in relationships and continue being "super." I discovered my superpowers as well as my weaknesses all came from the same place - inside of me. Stay with me for a minute.

I realized Superman and I had something in common - other than the cowlick in his hair, although mine was a widow's peak. There was a common trait that was quite the conundrum. The place that made him super also contained an element that made him ordinary. Kryptonite was a glowing green rock from his home planet that would strip away his powers if he encountered it. The closer he was to it, the weaker he became. I had more in common with this imaginary figure than I realized before. My power and abilities, as well as my hang-ups and weaknesses, could all be traced back to where I came from: not my natural geography but more succinctly, what was inside of me.

My Kryptonite wasn’t women, as I had once believed. It was deep-seated insecurities. I felt unfulfilled in relationships because my insecurities caused me to only seek validation without understanding why I needed it. And when you can’t articulate what you need, how can others provide it? Insecurities can also contribute to delusion in relationships where you arrogantly and foolishly believe you can do it alone. Help is what I needed but couldn't express it. Was it ego? Maybe. I tend to think it was passive aggressiveness. I believed my partners should have known what I needed in relationships whether I said it or not. In my mind, they were more consumed with what I could do for them, and what I needed didn’t matter. That was possibly true, but what I later found to be a fact was that in all my superpowers, I could not ask for help. There were times I did ask, but the pleas went ignored. Should couples consistently ask each other for help on the same thing, and if so, for how long?

Two examples of this come to mind. The first and funniest is from a portion of a Kevin Hart standup routine where he finds himself caught in a jam. He can't verbalize the situation, but he's looking at his best friend with a facial expression that means, *"Help me." "Help." "Me." "Niggah."* Have you been in a relationship with someone who saw you struggling and did nothing? They could see how heavy, tough, or challenging a situation was, and they just looked at you. Ohhhh...maybe they felt you could fix everything since you were so super and all. Meanwhile, every day you're looking at them like, *"Niggah... Help Me!"* LOL!

Maybe you're opposed to that word, so let's go with the next analogy. There is an expectation in relationships that when one partner sees the other in distress, they use their powers to help me (help us) to overcome the situation. Do we still believe in one for all and all for one? Whether the plea is with words or a facial expression, when the signal goes up, how do they respond? There is nothing like knowing that when you call for help, your partner, your lover, and your friend have your back.

The second example reverts to another of those '80s cartoon favorites of my era, *Thundercats*. Shame on you if you've never seen it. I'll cut to the good and most relevant part. Lion-O was the heir leader of this group of heroes that were variations of cats: Pantrho, Cheetara, and Tygra you get the point. Although Lion-O was chosen, he was the youngest and had to develop his senses, skills, and abilities as a warrior and leader. Relationships are not places we just show up in - there's always work to be done. Stick with me.

He carried a sword that was not only his weapon to fight with, but it also gave him insight and visions whenever danger was near. But the most important quality of this sword was that he could use it to summon the help of his friends when he needed it most, no matter where they were. *"Thunder Cats…Hoooo!"* This was the battle cry for help. He had great abilities but was at his best when those equipped to help him - both compatible and capable - also understood his call and were *willing* to help.

Before you discount my cartoon analogies as mere childhood fantasies, consider how practical these lessons become as adults. Every relationship has two people with superpowers. The key is to establish motives early and quickly when these relationships begin and to re-evaluate them often. Are you a friend or a foe? *"Are you here to help me or cause me harm?"* Wouldn't life be great if you could ask that simple of a question and get an honest answer? But it's not. Most foes will not admit their intentions. Unlike turning on a cartoon and immediately identifying the villain, relationships, and marriage usually require time and observation for ill intentions to surface. Foes can be those with the ability to help but for whatever reason refuse. There is no worse feeling than when your partner is capable but unwilling to help in a time of need.

This is why giving your blueprint too soon can be detrimental. Not only are you unaware of the other person's intentions, interests, or where their hearts may be, but you also don't know if their powers are compatible with yours. These are the special abilities that can make life together better or worse. The challenges in most relationships are knowing what the other's powers are and whether they choose to use their powers for good or evil.

When people in relationships have unresolved trauma, they tend to take revenge on their partners (oftentimes unknowingly) because of being unhealed and incomplete. They are like bombs ready to explode. You can recognize them because chaos and confusion follow them in every aspect of their life and relationships. Yet they refuse to be alone and rarely accept accountability to change their behavior. These people, unfortunately, get joy from making their partners miserable or find pleasure in their distress.

The real problem is that once they know what your Kryptonite is, they will often use it as leverage against you. Cries for help are futile, and if they do respond to your distress signal, it is usually to show how their powers are superior to yours. Have you ever had to muster the humility to ask your partner for money? A wife asking a husband is normal and common, right? But a husband asking a wife is unmanly, blasphemous, and unbiblical. What if the husband or wife are working multiple jobs and still need the assistance of their unwilling partner? Some superheroes are bad or have bad intentions and could be lying next to you every night.

Marital fizzle can result in partners who were once friends now becoming foes. As we saw in the example of Noah’s sons in the last chapter, a foe desires to expose their partner’s faults or weaknesses to others because it helps them appear as though they are better than their counterparts. If you have a partner who likes to loud-talk, is rude and disrespectful in public, or uses subtle tactics to show you they are in control, they have likely become a foe.

Hear me out; I’m not trying to break up “happy” homes, but what can be happy or harmonious about being in a relationship or married to someone committed to weakening you? Like Superman, the further you get away from people like this, the better chances you have of your mental, emotional, spiritual, and sometimes physical survival.

Another realization of couples is discovering that they don't know or realize they have powers or haven’t figured out how to use them well enough yet. This can be someone who has great potential in a relationship but needs some coaching and guidance. Like the first time you make love, and she whispers, *"That's the wrong spot."* Nothing a little coaching can't correct. That is unless he's on some other time and whispers back, *"Oh, I meant to go there."* LOL. In either scenario, this is the type of person with the willingness to figure it out and help. They may not have all the answers, but they have the heart to learn how to use the best of the powers they've been given and help you both succeed.

The next task is discerning the difference between capabilities and compatibilities. Yes, they have special abilities and are willing to use them for the good of your relationship, but what if it's in areas you don't need? This one may get a little dicey. This is when who they innately are and what they are gifted to do contrast with you and yours. An example could be that they are extraverted, and their gifts are greatly displayed interacting with people on every level. You, however, have extreme social anxiety and prefer the solitude of being at home, away from people.

These are the discoveries needed during dating to make the best life decisions. What this doesn't account for, though, and why it can be a touchy area, is what happens when there is a change of heart or compatibility. Something has changed. Instead of demonstrating the powers that attracted and connected you, your opposites no longer match.

Detecting this early in relationships makes it much easier for couples to navigate and decide their course versus those who have been married and are now miserable because of incompatibility. Barring any of the tragedies or traumas, marriage is supposed to be ’til death do you part. It’s the agreement to be supportive of each other’s process in hopes that you use your powers to help one another accomplish your goals - both individually and collectively. But what do you do with incompatibility? You relearn.

Discovering powers looks different than it did in the past. Our parents and grandparents didn’t use technology to socialize or as tools for learning and understanding people and the world around them - at least, mine didn’t. As I referenced earlier, lessons about life and relationships (good and bad) have been transferred from generation to generation. Self-discovery, however, looks different in this post-millennial society than it has in the past. First is having the mindset to want to change.

We get stuck in relationships when we refuse to assess ourselves and improve where needed. We believe and want our partners to stay the same. Nothing, including people, stays the same. Even superheroes must learn to adapt. If the skills on your job are no longer needed, you either retool and update your skillset, or you starve.

Superheroes must know who they are in addition to the powers they possess. Knowing who you are and what you're capable of can sometimes be the clarity needed to overcome compatibility issues in relationships. Who you are is not who you were, and it is not yet who you can become.

Several self-assessment and compatibility checks incorporate sciences that can be used to help better understand who we are and why we think and feel the way we do. That may not interest most people because to them it may seem unnecessary or pointless, especially if they've already gotten the girl or guy. But because the body and mind are constantly changing, it's imperative to know what your strengths are or where they may potentially grow.

If you've been married before, you already know how critical it is to know this about yourself and your partner. It becomes even more critical when/if you consider marriage again because what we do not learn, we are destined and doomed to repeat. Once you have learned the importance of compatibility, you should be mindful to reassess your powers often. The worst perspective to have been in is to believe that everyone else is the problem.

In reassessing your abilities, you should first see this as self-care. You can't be super for anyone else until you first discover what makes you super in the first place and be willing to recharge and reset. Men especially have a hard time doing this because (again) of how we are seen in society - both among ourselves and by women. The wrong partner - and possibly a foe - may tell you men don't need resets. My life experiences have shown me that if I don't find the reset, the reset will find me.

Altogether, I had been married for nearly 20 years of my life between two relationships and had to rediscover what it meant to take care of myself again. Basic strengths like running and managing a household for myself. I was reviving the skills to cook, clean, wash, dry, AND fold clothes and essentially take care of my functional day-to-day needs. (How many arguments have been had because the dryer is confused with a dresser? LOL).

To the untrained eye, these may seem like menial chores, but in a marriage, the willingness to manage these responsibilities requires keen abilities. Don't believe me? Married men, make it your business to do all the household chores for a few weeks and see what kinds of responses you get. She may even be willing to put her other superpowers to good use on you!

These are skills that make home life better and easier. You can indeed hire someone to do these things if you have the financial means to do so, but if not, something as simple as dinner, laundry, cleaning the house, paying bills, patience with the children, quality time, intimacy, and sex can all contribute to the Kryptonite that's killing the strength in a marriage.

The esteem I felt from saving the day was wasted every time I crashed and burned in a relationship, partly because I failed at home life. Yes, life is more than chores, but we must be able to see the value in the attentiveness of those needs closest to us. I failed to see that the place of deficiency - like my superpower - was also inside of me. I was the chief contributor to my demise and unhappiness by ignoring the areas in me that needed my attention. Like that dryer or chair filled with unfolded laundry, a sink full of dirty dishes, or unswept floors, my internal house needed to be cleaned. I finally turned a corner and was finding renewed purpose in doing simple things for myself again.

Like my childhood hero, I needed to escape the Kryptonite that rendered me powerless. The further I was able to get away from the mentalities that made me weak, the better I felt. I was also determined to ensure my insecurities would no longer be the indwelling Kryptonite that had sabotaged my thinking about relationships. Superman was back and black.

Although I wasn't sold on the thought of remarrying, I hadn't sworn it off with thoughts of becoming a monk in the Tibetan mountains.

I was finding my way and rediscovering myself. Clark Kent had blended into social life again, that is until he met Lois Lane. But Lois wasn't a damsel in distress who needed help. She had a different energy, almost as if she also was not from this planet.

I met my wife by "stumbling" into her DM. LOL. If you grew up with an 8-track in your car, allow me to explain. "DM" is a direct message sent to a person's private inbox. I say stumble because I was being nosey. One question led to another, and this is where the magic began. I would be hypocritical to say that although this was a blessed start for us, those "DMs" could also mean the Devil's Mindfill (DM) if you aren't careful. People's intentions behind direct messaging aren't always pure and can lead to regrettable circumstances. If you've ever received and answered an unexpected *"WYD"* message in your inbox, you already understand.

This is when I would cue the song every black old head that rides a bagger motorcycle plays while at a stop light. Roger Troutman and Zapp, *"Computer Love."* The voice box serenading a melody that has been used and sampled for decades now gives new meaning in our society today. It also connects with and calls to mind the words from another song called "Looking for love in all the wrong places." While there are horror stories of people who found nightmares while looking for fantasies, I'm grateful that was not my experience.

We exchanged messages for a while and finally agreed to meet in person, and that's when everything changed.

Chapter 10 – Keep the Fan On

No matter the temperature outside, keep the air circulating inside.

I experienced a eureka moment while messaging back and forth with my computer love. It seemed too good to be true. Down to our shared love for seafood, we had nearly everything in common, which was an impossibility considering what I had gone through. She was even a star basketball player in high school. I didn't officially play ball, but I was that dude on the blacktop. Meeting one another felt random and unexpected but as heart-pounding and exhilarating as if the game clock is winding down and you've got the ball in hand to take the last shot.

I learned that just when you think you have your sights and direction figured out, shifts happen, and this shift was as sudden and unpredictable as you can imagine. I wasn't looking for her and she wasn't looking for me. It was organic with the potential for fresh roots. But I was in no rush and had learned from my prior patterns and mistakes. So had she. We were both upfront about this and there were no brewing hopes or false expectations about our future lives together. We stayed in each moment and were content getting to know one another without being led by blueprints. It was genuine and authentic. Kudos to those who have always been able to be their authentic and unapologetic selves, but this was new and unchartered territory for a reformed pleaser.

I figured out a way to keep me from rushing into relationships quickly. I first believed being completely transparent about my past marriages would scare many away. But how do you handle someone who can see you for who you are? The ability to see beyond someone's representative is special. It's discernment. But it's also where many stop and ultimately fail at relationship building. It's not enough to see someone for who they are, but can you reach them? Can they reach you? Being able to touch them with gentleness and sincerity, however, is a gift. She was refreshingly unfamiliar. The way she spoke to me - how she looked at me - as if to say no matter what I previously experienced she was not moved or phased. It felt as if God used her to touch my heart to let me know everything would be ok and I no longer needed to fear being in a committed relationship. But I still was not ready to consider even the thought of marriage again.

The next few months seemed as if time had stood still, and after a few dates, I knew she was who I had been waiting for. As fine as she was, I would've given her an organ if she wanted it. But this is how I knew she was "her." We disagreed on how a situation could have been handled. It was minor and mild, but in my mind, the moment was a little spicy. I wasn't looking for reasons to be in a relationship, which would justify keeping my guard up and not allowing her to get any closer. I would chalk our chance encounter up as another dating experience and we would eventually move on.

Moments later it happened. She came back and acknowledged her part in the miscommunication and took full accountability. This was self-correction and self-awareness in real time. It wasn't her apology that got me, but rather her willingness to be the best version of herself - including the willingness to self-check. It was *emotional intelligence*. I had never seen this in real life, and it felt like a fresh wind. That small, forgettable exchange shifted my perspective on new possibilities with her. It also challenged me to be better; better at checking my pride and fixing mishaps now. She had me.

It was still vitally necessary that I resist the urge to be super and patiently wait for both our representatives to exit stage left. Experience taught me that this process cannot be rushed. I had learned that with or without a script (the blueprint) the representative can remain on stage but for so long. I told her I wanted us to be able to see each other in every season, twice. This wasn't about the Chronos time of two years or eight natural seasons. I was referring to the seasons of life.

What mental and emotional experiences do people have during the Fall and Spring (transitional) seasons of their lives – when people, relationships, money, joys, and pains all transition in or out of their lives? How do they behave or respond? Summer and Winter are the hottest and coldest climate seasons of the year. These translate to either the extremely joyful and carefree or the painful, isolated, and challenging moments in life. How do their moods shift around holidays or special occasions? How are they when dealing with the grief of losing a friend or loved one? Do they act differently around their family? How do they handle financial hardships? Are they different when they get a few coins?

Not only are these observations necessary in one set of seasons but should be regarded for at least two if considering marriage or remarriage. Some may not agree with this minimum two-year observation period, and it may sound hypocritical coming from a man who previously met and married someone in nine months. However, I will be the first to admit that it does not take long to know if someone is marriage material. But being marriage material versus knowing if it's the right fabric for you are two different realities. Within two years there is a baseline of consistent insight into each other's behaviors, patterns, and thought processes. You can observe how they show up in each season and determine if they match what you need.

Again, there are exceptions because every person and situation is different. This was the standard we followed, which allowed us both to see what we needed to see in one another. The observation period isn't to judge or fix how the other person may show up in these seasons. These are the opportunities to gain perspective about their wiring. The observation allows you to determine if they are a compatible, capable, AND willing match.

This is also a time in relationships that requires careful notetaking. You're not solely auditing for negative behaviors or looking for red flags. Truth is, you don't have to find flags, they reveal themselves. Instead, these are the good notes. These notes are the details about what makes them shine, smile, perk up, and smile uncontrollably. This practice set a precedence for the foundation of our relationship.

Let's say, all signs point to them being a perfect match. Not as perfect humans, but perfect in compatibility, capability, and willingness. Adam and Eve were flawed but chosen for one another to explore life together. Remember Big Mike? He and Alicia matured and considered a new future. Prince Hakeem and Lisa McDowell fell in love and moved back to Zumunda. But what did they observe about each other along the way? It turns out we were a perfect match through every season, and we paid close attention to the details.

Notes are essential in every relationship, especially in marriage. Whether you've been married a month or a "month of Sundays" mastering good notetaking could be the difference between Keith Sweat and Usher: making it last forever, or just letting it burn. Be sure to also examine your intentions as notetakers as well. Love keeps no record of wrongs, right? Do you keep more bad notes about your partner than good? You have pages of bad traits, bad habits, or bad decisions and not even three bullet points -worth of good. Remember this is your best friend, not your enemy. During our dating years, we noticed the simple gestures and moments that made each other smile. What gets your partner going, excited, and anxious…besides you know what?

Have you noticed how they respond to touch, affirmation, gifts, acts of service, or quality time spent together? Were you paying attention or did those notes get thrown away because at some point they failed to give you what you needed? Relationships can be hard, but they get worse when you no longer care about what makes your partner leap.

In this final chapter, I introduce a rarely quoted line from another *90's* cinema cult-classic movie, *"Love Jones,"* starring Larenz Tate (as Darius Lovehall) and Nia Long (as Nina Mosley).

The movie was a love story based on the culture of artistry and spoken word poetry. Darius is a spoken word artist and budding author who meets and is instantly attracted to Nina, a photographer who has just relocated to Chicago. The two "acquaint" and a romance ensues but is interrupted by, shall we say, circumstances (for the women that may not like my synopsis, find me on a podcast and let's argue). In one of the scenes, Darius's friend, Savon (played by Isaiah Washington) who, among their close-knit friends, is the only one married. Savon has recently separated from his wife, and Darius, amid his love issues with Nina, is encouraging him not to give up on their marriage and reminds him that he and his wife love each other. Savon's response was profound. He said, *"Falling in love ain't shit, somebody talk to me, please, about how to stay there."*

This is the chasm that started this book's journey from chapter One. Somebody, tell me how…

How do you keep the interest and fire blazing in your relationship and not become stagnant or complacent? Keep the fan on. How do you handle the compression of complaints, compound criticisms, and or aggregated attitudes between two lovebirds? Keep the fan on. How do you know if you've said or done enough to sustain your relationship? Enough may never be enough but keep the fan on.

How do you keep the cold out and heat in? Keep the fan on.

A few years ago, I started keeping the fan in my bedroom year-round because it helped with air circulation and regulated my body temperature. It was needed during the Summer and sweltering hot season. But surprisingly, it was just as effective during the winter months as well. The furnace heat during the night would cause me to have night sweats where I would be soaking wet by morning. The air circulated by the fan helped regulate my body temperature as I slept through the night – completely unaware of its effects.

Catch this in your Sha-Nah-Nah…as I come to my close:

The fan spinning above your head in your room is symbolic of the source above you needing to stay engaged in your relationship. First and always consult with God, through His Spirit, on how to use your fan appropriately for the best results in your relationship. Not praying for your mate, being attentive to their spiritual needs and desires, or hearing from God what they need from you as a partner would be like blowing on them on a hot summer day. You're trying but not using the right source.

Next, to get the best results you must know how to use your fan. Do you know what speed settings are wired into your relationship and which settings to use at the appropriate time? Sounds simple, but many have not been able to read their rooms successfully enough to know how to use the settings correctly. What do the low, medium, and high speeds feel like in different room temperatures? If your room is cold, putting the fan on high speed may not provide the level of comfort both of you need. But conversely, if the room is hot, a low speed won't cool it effectively. Low energy in a relationship could be just as useless as if the fan were not on at all. Men, this is one example where our testosterone and libido levels may have to be tested. Don't get her mouth all watery for some hash and all-you-have tuna in the cabinet. LOL (what movie is that from??)

Then, this is a big one because not many people realize this about their fans, make sure you have your fan set in the right direction. Your fan's function is optimal when it is turning in the direction that produces the appropriate type of airflow. I had to buy a ceiling fan to install in a room that didn't have one and found out when reading the directions that there is a button just below the base of the fan that changes the turning direction of the blades when it's on. The direction needed is based on the airflow needed for the room. If it's hot outside, the fan should be turning in one direction to keep the cooler air blowing and circulating; and when it's cold outside the opposite direction should be used to keep the warmer air flowing.

There are times in your relationship when the direction and settings you used in the summer won't work as well in the winter. When the heat in the relationship becomes uncomfortable and overwhelming, your fan will help keep fresh air flowing, if you use it right. But *"When it's cold outside…who are you hooolding?"* (speaking of Bobby Womack from chapter 5) The night cold is when it can feel the loneliest. Has your partner ever forbidden you from touching them in bed if your body was cold?

It may seem ridiculous or unnecessary to others to keep your fan on, but only you know what happens when it's not turned on. They don't know shit about your marriage. They don't know about the discomfort between you and your partner when the fan is not on. They don't know what it takes for your temperatures to be just right.

The notes you took become the fan settings for your room. If there are disagreements that are causing the room to become too hot or too cold use what you've learned to bring the room back to normal. Speak the language and use the fan settings appropriately. The wrong setting will make the room uncomfortable for you both.

Always remember the fan will never work without power. Please do not forget to make God the priority in your relationship. How do you do that? Pray and ask Him. It's just that simple. What makes it hard is when we refuse to listen to the answer, refuse to compromise and be reasonable, and refuse to grow together. If you're with the person, He designed you to be with know that what you need to be the best versions of yourselves for one another is inside of you. Find that place in one other that brings that day-one smile and tingle back. And whenever difficult seasons arise have each other's backs, front, and side. You are the earthly representation and reflection of God's eternal love for one another.

If you're thinking about marrying again at some point, good for you! Pray. Heal. Listen. Grow. And I can't forget, be patient. Let wisdom and peace guide you into your new next and may you find God's joy for your heart.

Finally, to every reader, despite your marital or dating status or happily married,

"Don't worry about anything; instead, pray about everything. Tell God what you need and thank him for all he has done. Then you will experience God's peace, which exceeds anything we can understand. His peace will guard your hearts and minds as you live in Christ Jesus."

Philippians 4:6-7 NLT

Epilogue

Have you ever slipped on Black Ice? It is a quick, sudden, and painful reality that you have fallen, yet the why and how it happened escapes you at that moment. It's generally not until you reflect on your environment's actual condition that you realize… "I should have seen this coming." We treat divorce and break-ups like black ice as if they happened out of nowhere. It's not until we find ourselves flat on our back, looking up at the sky, that we ask, "How did I get here?' The demise of marriages, much like black ice formation, requires certain weather conditions and environmental influences for it to show up. The climatic conditions have always been conducive to inclement weather events. The conditions we endure on this journey often leave us with scars and wounds that we tend to find ways to soothe and cover rather than fully allow them to heal.

Many times, we want to close a wound quickly so that it gives the *appearance* of being completely healed. The motive behind this is often aesthetics; we need it to look good even if it does not *feel* good. Some wounds need to heal from the inside out. This ensures that no germs and bacteria get trapped under the closed skin. Otherwise, while the outside looks intact, the inside is slowly destroyed. These types of wounds typically take longer to heal because they must be re-opened to address the core issue. The same is true in broken relationships until you work to heal the internal problems, individually and collectively. Otherwise, you will keep finding yourself needing to re-open unhealed places. Imagine how much further you and your mate could have progressed if you did not have to keep circling back to the same non-healing wound. Failure to address what is in the wound is the reason you remain uncomfortable, unsettled, and unfulfilled. With this, at some point, comes a sharp realization: you cannot ignore… *pain*.

The consistent accompaniment to unhealed wounds is pain, but I challenge you not to despise the pain you have endured, created, or encountered in your relationship journey. Pain is protective; as strange as that may sound, it has a purpose. When we feel pain, that pain is an indicator that something is wrong. Pain is protective because it warns us of further damage that may be pending; it is a symptom of an underlying issue. It will remind us that even when our mouths say, "I don't care," our actions will show the root of our problems. I believe we can agree that most people have a limit to how long they can ignore pain. In healthcare, pain was added as a vital sign to ensure it is being addressed the same way as with high blood pressure readings.

If you check your blood pressure and the reading is high, you understand that you need to take appropriate measures to lower it so that you decrease the risk of more serious complications like having a stroke. Pain in relationships must also be addressed as a priority to avoid disastrous complications. Different injuries in relationships cause varying degrees of pain, and how often you injure an area can increase or decrease the sensitivity. If you continue to cause or experience injury in a relationship or fail to address the pain, it is time to ask yourself if you want this to survive or if you need a reset.

Otherwise, the potential complications that may arise from ignored pain can be a matter of sanity vs insanity, peace vs turmoil, or life vs death. I pray that you choose to thrive and survive in the way that best fits where you are in life. The reset is not always a failure, nor is it always a divorce. A reset can come in the beautiful form of realignments, recommitment, and reconnection. A reset will always be an uncomfortable and sometimes painful pivot from an unwanted course. Prepare your hearts and minds to forgive yourself and perhaps your partner for the place of decision you have found yourself standing in. Facing relationship decisions often causes us to look back to the point of origin, and painful lookbacks can cause you to build resentment. Finding forgiveness will be the winning journey that, despite the old scars, opens the door to new possibilities of healing, hope, and peace.

In the Bible, we see Joseph finding success after surviving being placed in a pit by his brothers and sold into slavery, but even in finding success, he had to come face to face with his old wounds (his brothers). A part of the wonder of God is that He can use what broke you as the very thing you reencounter to show evidence of your healing. The road you have traveled to get to the point of being honest with yourself and your God may not be a road someone else wants to travel with you, and you must reconcile this within yourself. Inner reconciliation requires you to acknowledge falling short of what you intended, make peace with what you learned from the experience, and extend yourself the grace of forgiveness. Mastering these perspectives frees you from the weight of the opinions of others.

Truthfully, the road you have traveled to a place of loving and accepting your beautifully flawed self is not for everyone; it is just for the right one. Your next relationship's success depends heavily on your wholeness, honesty, and sometimes hard truths that the right partner will wholeheartedly welcome. Generally, roads crack and break because of weather conditions or overuse, or they are composed of unsuitable materials. A cracked or damaged road does not mean the journey ends; you only need to travel more carefully, but it can still lead you safely to your predetermined destination. Embracing the bumpy and pothole-laden roads has allowed us to fully appreciate where we currently stand as partners, lovers, and friends.

The trials and pivots of multiple marriages and divorces have helped me to fully respect that life's transitions can leave a person feeling frustrated, disappointed, and questioning God. (I know because I signed my autobiography). This book is not a self-righteous soapbox but a real-life story, sometimes messy, of how we almost settled without hope of finding real love and, at times, were big mad at God for our choices. I considered myself His favorite, but at one point in my life, I felt like He had left me to figure it out alone. We all know how it feels to have someone not meet our needs or expectations; this is generally when pride takes over, and we decide to do it ourselves.

I reached a point where I told God I would do it my way. Writing those chapters of my life was challenging, to say the least, and thinking back on it now, I felt like an untrained driver trying to win the Indy 500. But because of His grace, God helped me mature and pull back the layers to learn about myself through the DNA of my choices. I began to understand better why I made these decisions, dealt with my insecurities, and let go of the need to fit an image of what I thought successful relationships looked like.

After sifting through all my mess, mess-ups, and misguided choices, my honest reality was that I was reaping the outcomes of all the decisions I had made, the good, the bad, and the ugly. However, standing fully in that light allowed me to forgive myself, heal, and appreciate that even when I got off course, God's grace had already run ahead of me to settle the way.

I never imagined I would revere the broken road that led me to the peace and love my heart has after enduring two divorces. My best choice on my healing journey was to work on being better to myself than I had ever considered, and that started with unapologetic honesty. I clearly remember the long road that got me to this place, and I can see where God's hand guided, shielded, and chastised me along the way. It was not always what I prayed for, but after every questionable decision I made, it was just what I needed. It helped me stop worrying about my pit and whether I got pushed, tricked, or willfully jumped into the pit to give thanks for every protective pain God allowed along the way. The God I serve used the lowest places in my life as a footstool to elevate me toward the manifestation of His promises for me.

Our journey to marriage number three is not conventional and may have caused some not to complete this book. For others, our story may feel like a mockery of their desire to "hang in there." In the end, many may agree that we don't know Sh#% about marriage, but what we are sure of is that when we became a grounded and healed version of ourselves, a forever

LOVE found us. There is hope for experiencing an unfailing true partnership in love and life. Sometimes, the road traveled is not as scenic as we hoped, but for us, it was worth every lesson learned along the route to get to this destination.

Rascal Flats said it best: *"God blessed the broken road that led me straight to you."* This journey through the complexities of relationships, marriage, divorce, and the blending of family has validated a mantra I wholeheartedly believe: *Just because you started late does not mean you won't finish on time.*

Nikimi Lyles, RN

#Lovewins
#Giveitafightingchance

Final Note from the Author

If you were unsure what to expect from this book based on the title, hopefully, you better understand my story. This is more than a catchy phrase to sell books but the rawness of the journey with many blemishes.

Thank you for buying the book and for reading through to the end. Whether you are in a great relationship, marriage, are happily content in singleness, or are in a season of uncertainty about it all, I hope there was something in my story that has helped in some way. Maybe it provided insight, gave a different perspective, or made you laugh. My story, my journey, is mine and yours is yours. Only you and God know the state and condition of your relationship and what is needed to make it grow. Some will plant and some will water, but God will increase. *1 Corinthians 3:6.*

Prayerfully this was either; the seed to start fresh in self-reflection and insight in planting new thoughts and ideas to grow your relationships; or some refreshing water to remind you how common struggles and pains of relationships are, but that recovery is possible. God gives the increase. He allows the grace, compassion, and love to look within

Humans are imperfect and their relationships will be also. Perfection is not the goal, agreement is. Here are two principles my wife and I have agreed to that have changed our lives: an attitude of gratitude and regular check-ins.

Honest answers only: Would your partner respond differently, better, if they knew how much and how often they are appreciated? How do you show appreciation? Do they accept (positively respond) to the appreciation you give? If not, make sure you are speaking their languages. I encourage you to also read *The Five Love Languages* by Gary Chapman if you haven't already. And if you have, read it again.

One of the key points I believe couples miss is that it's about identifying *your* love language. The book essentially guides you in exploring *your partner's* love languages. This could be the reason they don't respond or react to certain gestures of love. You could be demonstrating how you want to be appreciated versus the language they need. This is a resource to identify compatibility as well.

The next principle my wife and I agreed to is regular and open check-ins. This one may be tough for men, particularly with being transparent and honest. Truth be told, while women need to feel safe and secure in a relationship, men have the same need as well. Open and transparent communication is viewed by some as a weakness, and many men avoid this space. Sharing inner thoughts and emotions for both men and women can feel unsafe depending on the responsiveness of their partners. Reassure one another that thoughts and feelings are welcomed, honored, and respected. There is an adage that couples should learn to "fight fair" in relationships. But when check-ins are done openly, honestly, and regularly, you likely won't have to "fight" at all.

For a check-in to be successful, couples must intentionally engage in conversation about where they are and what (if anything) is needed from the other. I remember the first time my wife asked, *"What do you need from me?"* The probing sincerity of her question left me void of words. I didn't know how to respond other than to say, *"I'm good.... what do you need from me?"* I learned this was more than a question. It was her way of examining herself through my expectations, and she would do whatever in her power to make that happen.

She knew I would do the same. Success in relationships is achieving a common goal. While you are responsible for your happiness, when you and your partner commit to being the best versions of yourselves for one another, you win.

These principles set the foundation of our forever love. Every day we make the conscious decision to love each other better than the day before. Being grateful for our journeys and how God allowed our paths to cross, in the respective seasons of our lives, gave us a deeper appreciation for His Sovereignty. We would not have been able to make this story up in a thousand lifetimes, but the traumas, pains, scars, and roller coasters were worth it. We passionately work to grow and develop our relationship. What good is being grateful for God's gift if you aren't willing to do the work to cultivate and take care of it?

Win in your relationships no matter what and at all costs – whenever possible. That's the message - as contradicting as it may sound considering the "whenever possible" part. The statistical reality is half or most marriages may fail. It doesn't mean you are a failure, just that the connection could not last. But what does a lasting relationship mean? Does it mean we grow tolerant of one another until one of us dies? Unfulfilled. Undesirable. Or is it a picturesque idea of holding hands, kissing, and still chasing each other around with our walkers and canes at 90? If we're honest most if not all couples marry with that ideal expectation in mind.

Unfortunately, there are unplanned deviations from that plan and, at times, unexpected exceptions that must be made – especially when personal safety and well-being are at stake. Another layered meaning, or message within the message is if you are in an abusive relationship get out and get professional help. God will heal the broken spirit of both the victim and abuser if they are willing. But the natural person also needs guidance and a pathway to physical, mental, and emotional healing as well.

There is a hopeful tomorrow for those who have experienced brokenness due to relationships and marriage. As I pray this prayer, be open to how God, through His Spirit, can move in your life. If you don’t believe in God or prayer, I sincerely hope whatever faith you have been given leads you to Him and His love.

Heavenly Father, I pray for hearts that are seeking you for wisdom and guidance about their lives and relationships. Only you know the inner thoughts and details of every person’s situation. Please grant them grace and compassion for the person you have blessed them with. Open their eyes to see one another the way you see them. Open their hearts to love them the way you them. Open their minds to understand and not just to be understood. I pray for unity and strength. I pray for never-ending love and ideas and ways to continuously love each other better.

For those in their season of singleness, give them strength as well to endure. If they are parents, give them the wisdom and grace to parent effectively despite past hurts. Heal their hearts and help them avoid passing those hurts to their children. If they have a desire to find love again, prepare their mind and hearts that will make room for their designed person.

Keep us from self-sabotage help us renew our minds and manage the gifts you have given to us. Help us be mindful that we are reflections of you and our relationships model your truth and love to all. May we be diligent, committed, and faithful to you and each other until our days are no more.

I pray this in the power of Yeshuah's name.

Amen.

About the Author

Christopher Lyles, Sr. has lived most of his life by the motto, *"Control what you can control and let God handle the rest."* He has a nearly three-decade career in corporate technology and just as many years as an ordained minister. However, as a first-time author, he taps into a different familiarity. He is also a two-time divorcee.

In his first book, *Don't Ask Me Sh%! About Marriage,* Chris shares the impacts divorce and remarriage have had on his life and faith. While he doesn't consider himself a relationship expert, he jokingly says, *"Based on my relationship track record, some may say that I'm an expert at getting them [relationships] wrong."*

Despite his failures in marriage, Chris believes in the foundational principles of marriage and the value and stability it has in our societal structure. To find out what keeps him so optimistic visit his websites for more insight, podcasts, merchandise, and giveaways:
www.DontAskMeAboutMarriage.com

The End

Made in the USA
Coppell, TX
27 June 2026

83604392R00098